Edinburgh

DIRECTIONS

WRITTEN AND RESEARCHED BY

Donald Reid

NEW YORK • LONDON • DELHI

www.roughguides.com

Contents

Introduction to

Edinburgh

Laid out over a series of volcanic crags, its jagged skyline of domes, turrets and spires topped by an impregnable castle, few European cities can boast Edinburgh's dramatic impact. Cobbled medieval closes, steep stairways and hidden courtyards make up its labyrinthine Old Town, while a few hundred metres to the north wide thoroughfares and grand Neoclassical facades characterize the city's eighteenth-century New Town. Together they constitute a World Heritage Site – a historic treasure that's also the heart of the living, working city.

With tightly packed tenement houses alongside faux Venetian palaces and dynamic contemporary constructions set against wide-open acres of parkland, Edinburgh is a compellingly theatrical place – awash with history yet, in places, refreshingly modern, and as thick with pomp and grandeur as it is intimate and friendly. Its centre is remarkably compact, and the majority of the main sights are within easy walking distance of each other. The city is also characterized by extensive green spaces: you can climb to the top of Arthur's Seat to look over Edinburgh and its suburbs, walk along

When to visit

Edinburgh's typically British climate means a clear seasonal divide between frost- and snow-tinged winters, blustery and colourful springs, warm (but rarely hot) summers and golden, then gloomy, autumns. The east-coast location ensures slightly less rainfall than western Scotland, though sharp and sometimes bitter winds blow in off the North Sea. The coldest months are January and February, with an average daily temperature of 6°C; in July the average is 18°C; late spring (May) and early autumn (Sept) are often good times to visit, offering welcome spells of bright weather and less of the high season's tourist scrum. With the Festival in full swing, August is perhaps the most exciting time to be in Edinburgh, though be prepared for huge crowds.

the gentle Water of Leith, or stand by the breezy shores of the Firth of Forth and admire the gigantic geometric girders of the Forth Rail Bridge.

Edinburgh's status as Scottish capital has endowed it with an outstanding collection of national institutions, from museums and magnificent art collections to a controversial but intriguing new parliament building, as well as a host of more populist attractions that include the former Royal Yacht *Britannia* and the world's best indoor climbing facility. And while the city is rich in heritage, it's also confident in its role as a thoroughly modern European capital and an important centre of finance and research. The prevailing conservatism is cast aside both in the flair of the annual Festival, which transforms Edinburgh into a giant celebration of the arts and entertainment, and in the hedonism of the New Year party, Hogmanay, when thousands of revellers throng the streets and the skies explode with fireworks. Theatres, live-music venues and art galleries provide rich cultural pickings throughout the year, while the old wood-lined pubs, cosmopolitan cafés and clubs, dramatic rooftop restaurants and busy seafood bistros provide all the evidence you need of a city charged with spirit and life among its old stones.

Edinburgh
AT A GLANCE

OLD TOWN

This is the core of historic Edinburgh, with the centrepiece Royal Mile and its string of key attractions running east from the castle down to Holyrood, home of the royal palace and startling modern parliament. The tangled passageways and courtyards which lead off the Mile are far less touristy, and remain evocative of the area's medieval character.

New Town houses

NEW TOWN

A masterpiece of early town planning, with row upon elegant row of impressive Georgian houses intermixed with haughty Neo classical monuments, the New Town's oldest quarter has been colonized by department stores and offices. Explore further and you'll discover attractive residential enclaves as well as bohemian Broughton, the focus of Edinburgh's gay scene.

Ramsay Gardens, Old Town

LEITH

The port of Edinburgh, Leith is just as historic as the city – if rather less well preserved and fringed by some grim housing estates. The old harbour, however, now holds some fine restaurants, while the redeveloped former docklands are the retirement home of that epitome of the British establishment, the Royal Yacht *Britannia*.

Leith's waterfront

WATER OF LEITH

Little more than a meandering stream, the Water of Leith threads its way through the suburbs in the north of the city, with an accompanying walkway offering a verdant, leafy passage between non-touristy districts such as Stockbridge, Inverleith and Dean Village.

HOLYROOD PARK

Just half a mile from the city centre, this vast public park covers as large an area as the Old and New Towns combined. Mostly made up of rough, hilly terrain that offers some terrific walks, it incorporates the 823 metre peak of Arthur's Seat as well as the striking Salisbury Crags cliffs.

◄ Water of Leith

► Holyrood Park

Ideas

The big six

Part of the pleasure of visiting Edinburgh is in simply wandering with no fixed agenda, through narrow closes and up vertiginous steps, past windswept viewpoints or along the grand avenues of the New Town. But there are some landmark sights that you really shouldn't miss. These encapsulate what's great about Scotland's capital, where history, heritage and dramatic views mix with impressive buildings from many eras.

▲ Museum of Scotland

An intriguing piece of contemporary architecture that's a worthy home for Scotland's national historic treasures.

P.88 ▸ SOUTH OF THE ROYAL MILE

▼ Scottish Parliament

Overflowing with imagery, quirky design and controversy, and now one of the city's star attractions.

P.80 ▸ HOLYROOD AND ARTHUR'S SEAT

▶ The Royal Mile

One of the world's most famous streets, with every cobbled inch echoing the hurly-burly of Edinburgh past and present.

P.63 ▸ THE ROYAL MILE

▼ Edinburgh Castle

This mighty historic fortress, perched atop its impregnable rock: admire it from afar or explore from within.

P.63 ▸ THE ROYAL MILE

▲ Forth Rail Bridge

The gigantic girders of this iconic monument to Victorian engineering span the Firth of Forth just northwest of Edinburgh.

P.152 ▸ SOUTH QUEENSFERRY AND THE FORTH BRIDGES

▼ Calton Hill

Studded with an odd collection of Neoclassical architecture, this is the best of many great viewpoints from which to gaze out over the city.

P.114 ▸ CALTON HILL AND BROUGHTON

Edinburgh Festival

The Edinburgh Festival is one of the greatest shows on earth, a month of cultural gluttony and mind-boggling artistic activity. Every performance space – from the grandest concert halls to pub courtyards – plays host to a packed programme of arts and entertainment, ranging from orchestral performances to stand-up comedy, ground-breaking theatre to avant-garde cinema. Whether you're dashing around a dozen shows in a day or checking out the street performers, Edinburgh in August is an essential experience.

▲ **Fireworks concert**

This spectacular and free Festival climax lights up the night sky above the castle.

P.177 ▸ ESSENTIALS

▲ **International Festival**

This highbrow event draws world-class orchestras, choirs, dance and theatre companies to Edinburgh.

P.177 ▸ ESSENTIALS

◀ The Fringe

The Fringe office becomes a hive of activity during the festival, when venues throughout the city showcase around 1500 performances a day.

P.177 ▸ ESSENTIALS

▼ Street theatre

During the Festival the Royal Mile becomes one elongated stage for buskers and street performers from all over the world.

P.176 ▸ ESSENTIALS

◀ Comedy

A successful Fringe stand-up show is the benchmark of success for almost every comedian in Britain.

P.177 ▸ ESSENTIALS

▶ Edinburgh International Book Festival

This hugely popular fortnight features readings, discussions and interviews with well-known authors.

P.178 ▸ ESSENTIALS

Royal Edinburgh

The monarch need not be at her official Edinburgh residence for the capital to adopt the trappings of a royal city. The lives of the Stewarts (six kings named James, plus Mary, Queen of Scots) were intricately involved with Edinburgh for centuries – and it was from Holyrood that James VI departed for London to unite the thrones of Britain. Today, the castle secures Scotland's crown jewels and coronation stone, while Leith harbours that most quintessential emblem of the British royalty abroad, the Royal Yacht *Britannia*.

▲ Royal Yacht Britannia

Now enjoying dignified retirement in Leith, *Britannia* offers an intriguing insight into Britain's recent royal heritage.

P.131 ▸ LEITH

▶ Thistle Chapel, High Kirk of St Giles

This beautiful side-chapel is used by the Queen to install Knights of the Thistle, the highest chivalric order in Scotland.

P.69 ▶ THE ROYAL MILE

◀ Edinburgh Castle

The castle's permanent military garrison helps guard the "Honours", or crown jewels, of Scotland.

P.63 ▶ THE ROYAL MILE

▲ Queen's Gallery

Precious art and artefacts from the rarely seen Royal Collection are displayed in this attractive small gallery at Holyrood.

P.80 ▶ HOLYROOD AND ARTHUR'S SEAT

▶ Palace of Holyroodhouse

An impressive introduction into the lives and loves of the Scottish kings and queens.

P.77 ▶ HOLYROOD AND ARTHUR'S SEAT

Theatre and music

Thankfully, Edinburgh's cultural life doesn't shut down for the eleven months of the year that the city spends recovering from the Festival. An array of excellent venues, some serious local talent and a deeply embedded appreciation of music, song and performance combine to ensure an impressive variety of theatre and music across the city year-round, from touring performances of the Royal Shakespeare Company to an impromptu folk or jazz session.

▲ The Lot

This converted church in the historic Grassmarket plays host to the city's most dynamic line-up of local and touring modern jazz acts.

P.174 ▶ ESSENTIALS

▲ Festival Theatre

The prime place in town for national and international ballet and opera performances.

P.175 ▶ ESSENTIALS

▲ Traverse Theatre

Consistently impressive, staging ground-breaking new writing and innovative contemporary drama.

P.175 ▸ ESSENTIALS

▼ Sandy Bell's

A small traditional pub, where friends with fiddles tend to meet – and invariably strike up a tune or two.

P.174 ▸ ESSENTIALS

▶ Usher Hall

The city's dignified old concert hall hosts the world's top orchestras as well as big-name rock and pop acts.

P.174 ▸ ESSENTIALS

Medieval Edinburgh

Few European capitals have preserved the medieval era so resonantly as Edinburgh, both in religious buildings such as Rosslyn Chapel and ruined Holyrood Abbey, and in the haphazard layout of the Old Town itself. With its narrow passageways off the Royal Mile leading to tightly packed tenement houses which rise a giddying eight or nine storeys, a wander through the cobbled streets here can take you straight back through the centuries.

▲ Inchcolm

This tranquil island holds Scotland's finest original medieval abbey, and affords sweeping views back to Edinburgh.

P.153 ▶ SOUTH QUEENSFERRY AND THE FORTH BRIDGES

▲ Holyrood Abbey

These atmospheric remains are a poignant memorial to the destructive religious wars which dominated medieval Scotland.

P.79 ▶ HOLYROOD AND ARTHUR'S SEAT

▲ Gladstone's Land

The best preserved of the Royal Mile's tenements, this creaking, dark building gives a glimpse of day-to-day life in the medieval city.

P.67 ▶ THE ROYAL MILE

▼ Rosslyn Chapel

The cryptic Biblical carvings and secretive symbols in this intriguing fifteenth-century church play a key role in the *Da Vinci Code* and other historical-religious conspiracies.

P.146 ▶ SOUTH EDINBURGH

◀ Grassmarket and Victoria Street

Tall tenements crowd around this rough-and-tumble Old Town quarter, notable for its quirky shops and friendly pubs.

P.85 ▶ SOUTH OF THE ROYAL MILE

▼ Canongate Kirk

This gracefully simple seventeenth-century church boasts the city's most attractive historic graveyard.

P.72 ▶ THE ROYAL MILE

Dead Edinburgh

There's a distinctly sinister and macabre edge to Edinburgh's history, and if you join a tour of the old cemeteries or walk through the narrow corridors of the Old Town after dusk, you're bound to absorb some of this rather creepy atmosphere. The dead are given life here in less spooky ways, too, whether through the legions of visitors who research the details of long-forgotten ancestors in Edinburgh's archives, or by supping a few drinks near the site of the city's old gallows.

▼ Greyfriars Bobby statue

Edinburgh's most sentimental statue, honouring the loyal terrier who watched over his master's grave for fourteen years.

P.88 ▶ SOUTH OF THE ROYAL MILE

▼ The Last Drop Tavern

This convivial pub pays tribute to the public hangings which once took place across the road.

P.96 ▶ SOUTH OF THE ROYAL MILE

THE LAST DROP

▶ Surgeon's Hall Museum

A wonderfully macabre museum dedicated to surgery, anatomy and pathology.

P.91 ▶ SOUTH OF THE ROYAL MILE

▲ Calton Old Burial Ground

A wealth of intriguing gravestones and memorials to citizens both famous and obscure.

P.114 ▶ CALTON HILL AND BROUGHTON

◀ Ancestor research

Clamber around your family tree via the extensive resources of the General Register Office, the National Archives of Scotland and the National Library.

P.97 ▶ ALONG PRINCES STREET

◀ Ghost tours

Let costumed characters lead you on spine-tingling visits to the graveyards and haunted corners of Edinburgh's underworld.

P.66 ▶ THE ROYAL MILE

Literary Edinburgh

Edinburgh's status as UNESCO's first World City of Literature is testament to the writers, poets and publishers who have moulded its prominent literary culture. Famous sons of the city such as Sir Walter Scott and Robert Louis Stevenson enjoy numerous memorials and references around Edinburgh, while literary tours allow you to follow up local links with many other characters and authors, from Sherlock Holmes and Harry Potter to Irvine Welsh and Ian Rankin.

▲ McNaughtan's bookshop

The best of the city's secondhand book-shops, stacked high with well-thumbed novels and pristine first editions.

P.118 ▶ CALTON HILL AND BROUGHTON

▼ Scott Monument

This huge Gothic rocket on Princes Street commemorates Sir Walter Scott, author of *Ivanhoe* and the Waverley novels.

P.100 ▶ ALONG PRINCES STREET

THE EDINBURGH LITERARY PUB TOUR

▲ Literary pub tour

A convivial jaunt in words and whisky around the pubs frequented by the city's famous writers.

P.66 ▸ THE ROYAL MILE

▲ Writers' museum

Reams of memorabilia relating to Edinburgh's greatest literary giants: Walter Scott, Robert Louis Stevenson and Robert Burns.

P.68 ▸ THE ROYAL MILE

▼ Elephant House

One of the Old Town cafés where J.K. Rowling sought a warm corner to scribble the first Harry Potter story.

P.93 ▸ SOUTH OF THE ROYAL MILE

▼ Oxford Bar

Still unspoiled, this is the preferred drinking spot of both Inspector Rebus and his creator, Ian Rankin.

P.113 ▸ THE NEW TOWN

Galleries and museums

In its art galleries and museums, Edinburgh has all the wealth and privilege of a capital city, with Scotland's finest art and artefacts presented in a series of impressive buildings. The national collections here are not daunting in size, with most relatively easy to digest in an hour or two's viewing, and entry to almost all is free. Venture beyond them, and you'll also find a rich, varied range of private and commercial galleries showcasing vibrant contemporary talent.

▲ Fruitmarket Gallery

The city's most dynamic exhibition space, devoted to changing exhibitions of international 21st century art.

P.99 ▸ ALONG PRINCES STREET

▲ National Gallery of Scotland

Intimate and inspiring galleries displaying works by Botticelli, Titian, Rembrandt, the Impressionists and Scotland's finest pre-twentieth-century artists.

P.101 ▸ ALONG PRINCES STREET

▼ Dean Gallery

Taking up two whole storeys, Paolozzi's massive *Vulcan* is the highlight of this superb collection of modern art.

P.125 ▸ ALONG THE WATER OF LEITH

▲ National Museum of Scotland

This imaginatively designed modern building holds Scotland's premier collection of historic artefacts.

P.88 ▸ SOUTH OF THE ROYAL MILE

▶ Royal Museum of Scotland

Part of the National Museum, this airy iron-framed nineteenth-century palazzo houses a vast range of antiquities from around the world.

P.89 ▸ SOUTH OF THE ROYAL MILE

◀ Dundas Street galleries

A concentrated series of private and commercial galleries, many specializing in local contemporary artists.

P.108 ▸ THE NEW TOWN

Sports and activities

Edinburgh's contribution to the history of sport is unexpectedly significant: the rules of golf were drawn up in Leith, while the world's first ever rugby international was played on a local cricket ground. Today, rugby internationals at Murrayfield are colourful, passionate events; if participation is more your thing, head for the world's largest indoor climbing arena, or take to Edinburgh's many green spaces, which are perfect for jogging, cycling, walking or even flying a kite.

▲ EICA:Ratho

The Edinburgh International Climbing Arena has some world-class indoor climbing facilities.

P.140 ▸ NORTH AND WEST EDINBURGH

▼ Arthur's Seat

The open green spaces of Holyrood Park offer walkers an inviting taste of the rugged Scottish Highlands.

P.83 ▸ HOLYROOD AND ARTHUR'S SEAT

▶ Rugby

Played in front of noisy crowds of 65,000, Scotland's home international fixtures are usually stirring encounters.

P.138 ▶ NORTH AND WEST EDINBURGH

▼ Golf

Edinburgh has numerous excellent places to play, including a number of accessible public and short-hole courses.

P.182 ▶ ESSENTIALS

▲ Loony Dook

The traditional South Queensferry way to welcome the New Year is a swim in the Firth of Forth. It's not compulsory, but it is cold.

P.150 ▶ SOUTH QUEENSFERRY AND THE FORTH BRIDGES

Traditional pubs

It's often said that if the weather in Scotland was any better, the pubs wouldn't be so good. Edinburgh has more than its fair share of classic venues, from low-beamed rooms tucked into Old Town basements to splendid Victorian bars graced with ornate cornicing and magnificent tiled walls. And it's not just whisky that flows freely – Edinburgh also has a long tradition as a centre of beer brewing.

▲ Jolly Judge

A tiny pub tucked away in a hidden court-yard just off the oldest part of the Royal Mile.

P.76 ▸ THE ROYAL MILE

▲ Bow Bar

An unaffected champion of Edinburgh's old-style bars, with a lip-smacking range of real ales and single malt whiskies.

P.95 ▸ SOUTH OF THE ROYAL MILE

▼ Sheep Heid Inn

The highlight of the urban village of Duddingston is this local pub and its old-fashioned skittle alley.

P.84 ▶ HOLYROOD AND ARTHUR'S SEAT

▲ Café Royal Circle Bar

A magnificent listed interior featuring mahogany carvings and hand-painted tiles, as well as good food and beer on tap.

P.104 ▶ ALONG PRINCES STREET

◀ Cumberland Bar

A discerning choice for a beer and good conversation in the New Town

P.113 ▶ THE NEW TOWN

▼ The Shore

This wood- and mirror-lined haunt abuts the water in Leith's old harbour.

P.135 ▶ LEITH

Classical Edinburgh

Planned and built in the eighteenth century, Edinburgh's elegant New Town offered a unique opportunity for Classically-influenced architects of the time to bring grandeur and magnificence to the cityscape. Edinburgh was soon dubbed the "Athens of the North", and construction of a mock-Parthenon on Calton Hill began; this half-completed monument may still be known as "Edinburgh's Disgrace", but the Classical legacy elsewhere in the city is quite the opposite.

▼ St Bernard's Well

This elegant Doric rotunda adds an Arcadian aspect to the Water of Leith.

P.121 ▶ ALONG THE WATER OF LEITH

▼ Georgian House

A National Trust for Scotland property furnished to show off the grandeur of early nineteenth century living.

P.108 ▶ THE NEW TOWN

▶ Hopetoun House

Scotland's grandest stately home is a magnificent tribute to the Neoclassical vision of the Adam family of architects.

P.151 ▶ SOUTH QUEENSFERRY AND THE FORTH BRIDGES

▲ Calton Hill

The strange collection of nineteenth-century buildings and memorials here include the unfinished National Monument.

P.114 ▶ CALTON HILL AND BROUGHTON

◀ New Town

One of Europe's finest residential quarters, with rows and terraces of dignified Georgian architecture.

P.105 ▶ THE NEW TOWN

▶ National Gallery of Scotland

One of two Grecian temples built right in the heart of the capital to house Scotland's collection of art treasures.

P.101 ▶ ALONG PRINCES STREET

Restaurants

Edinburgh's restaurant scene is as appealing as anywhere else in the UK outside London. Not only is there a vast choice of places, at the top end you can encounter Michelin-starred chefs, some memorable eating spaces and a range of distinctive dining experiences. Scotland's seafood, beef and venison is world-class produce, and is imaginatively utilized by chefs to create a unique style of modern Scottish cuisine.

▲ The Grain Store

An understated interior and an impressive Scottish menu make this a great place for a casual but sophisticated meal.

P.94 ▸ SOUTH OF THE ROYAL MILE

▼ The Boathouse

Some of the best seafood in the Edinburgh area, served with wonderful views across the Forth to the mighty road and rail bridges.

P.154 ▸ SOUTH QUEENSFERRY AND THE FORTH BRIDGES

Welcome to
the
Boat House

Fresh Sea Food

LICENCED RESTAURANT

◄ The Vintner's Rooms

An elegant, charming and historic dining space complemented by top-notch Scottish-French cooking.

P.134 ► LEITH

► The Kitchin

The most dynamic young restaurant in Edinburgh, boasting an excellent menu of Scottish produce and, within months of opening, a Michelin star.

P.134 ► LEITH

▼ blue

Located in the heart of theatreland, this slick but friendly bistro sources many ingredients from the nearby farmers' market.

P.94 ► SOUTH OF THE ROYAL MILE

▼ David Bann's

One of Edinburgh's hippest places to eat, with a varied and interesting meat-free menu.

P.75 ► THE ROYAL MILE

Hidden Edinburgh

Edinburgh is so full of important buildings and grand architecture that in the procession from one to the other it's easy to overlook the city's less obvious draws. Yet there are many hidden corners – not just in the Old Town, where there seem to be secrets down every close and even under the ground, but also out from the centre, where ancient villages hold onto their identity despite having been subsumed into the capital.

▲ Vaults tour

Take a tour of the town below the ground to discover the city's catacombs, vaults and subterranean passageways.

P.66 ▸ THE ROYAL MILE

▲ The Witchery by the castle

There's an other-worldliness to the charming Secret Garden, part of a gothic-themed fine dining restaurant hidden away near the castle.

P.76 ▸ THE ROYAL MILE

◀ Mary King's Close

Edinburgh's "lost city" is a remarkably well-preserved series of Old Town houses and closes in the basement of the City Chambers.

P.70 ▶ THE ROYAL MILE

▼ Dean Village

This charming, secluded little community of converted mill buildings is one of the landmarks on the Water of Leith Walkway.

P.124 ▶ ALONG THE WATER OF LEITH

◀ Dunbar's Close Garden

Tucked down a Royal Mile close, this tiny formal garden is an inspiring and tranquil retreat from the bustling city centre.

P.72 ▶ THE ROYAL MILE

Gourmet Edinburgh

Edinburgh has a long history when it comes to a taste for the good things in life. The revered Valvona & Crolla deli opened here in 1934, while whisky merchants such as William Cadenhead have been around since the nineteenth century. Both remain star attractions of the city's impressive range of gourmet experiences, specialist food shops and delicatessens, which also includes a regular farmers' market, showcasing produce from in and around the city.

▲ Iain Mellis Cheesemonger

With three shops piled high with rounds of delicious British and continental cheeses, Mr Mellis is well worth sniffing out.

P.92 ▸ SOUTH OF THE ROYAL MILE

▲ Farmers' market

The best local meat, fish, cheese, bread and vegetables sold in the shadow of the castle.

P.92 ▸ SOUTH OF THE ROYAL MILE

▲ Valvona & Crolla

Possibly the finest Italian deli in Britain, this is a truly inspiring emporium of the finest fresh foods, fine wines and epicurean treats.

P.118 ▶ CALTON HILL AND BROUGHTON

▼ Cadenhead's

This small, unassuming shop sells a bewildering range of whiskies, including many rare and specially bottled distillations.

P.73 ▶ THE ROYAL MILE

▶ Falko Konditormeister

Beautifully crafted and wonderfully tasty cakes, breads and confectionery created by a German-trained master baker.

P.147 ▶ SOUTH EDINBURGH

Clubs and style Bars

Edinburgh's vibrant nightlife scene covers all the genres, from dub to disco and chillout to comedy, but the most memorable aspect of a night out here is the range and variety of venues. The "style bars" try to outdo their competitors with up-to-the-minute design, while others make the most of ornate former banks and offices, and clubs occupy ever more unusual locations, with nights staged in old churches, smart Georgian mansions and even the Royal Mile's vaults.

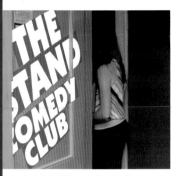

▲ Stand Comedy Club

Edinburgh's top venue for stand-up keeps the giggles going seven days a week, twelve months a year.

P.175 ▸ ESSENTIALS

▲ Cabaret Voltaire

The Old Town's catacombs provide a unique venue for some of the city's top DJs.

P.173 ▸ ESSENTIALS

▲ Tigerlily

The flashiest place to be seen sipping pink champagne on Edinburgh's glitz strip, George Street.

P.113 ▸ THE NEW TOWN

▲ Cruz

A floating bar, restaurant and nightclub that looks the part after a lavish recent makeover.

P.134 ▸ LEITH

▲ The Dome

This stunning cocktail bar and restaurant in a converted bank is a sophisticated spot for a drink or meal.

P.113 ▸ THE NEW TOWN

◀ Dragonfly

Small but definitively hip hangout near the Grassmarket with chandeliers, clever cocktails and cool wallpaper.

P.96 ▸ SOUTH OF THE ROYAL MILE

Gay Edinburgh

For all Edinburgh's reputation as a dour, stern, Calvinist city, the gay quarter here is well-established in bohemian Broughton on the edge of the New Town. In addition to a number of gay cafés, bars and nightclubs, most of them straight-friendly and a familiar part of the social circuit, there are stylish gay-run guesthouses and colourful annual events celebrating the gay community in Scotland.

▲ Blue Moon Café

The city's longest-established and best-known gay café, right in the heart of things off Broughton Street.

P.119 ▶ CALTON HILL AND BROUGHTON

▶ Ardmor House

This gay-owned guesthouse ranks among the most contemporary and stylish small places to stay in Edinburgh.

P.164 ▶ ACCOMMODATION

▲ CC Blooms

Edinburgh's sole uniquely gay nightclub is always loud, lively and popular.

P.174 ▶ ESSENTIALS

▶ Planet Out

One of the main meeting points of Edinburgh's gay scene, this drinking spot rocks as a busy pre-club bar.

P.120 ▶ CALTON HILL AND
BROUGHTON

◀ Pride Scotia festival

Annual parade and celebration held on alternate years in Edinburgh and Glasgow.

P.180 ▶ ESSENTIALS

Indulgent Edinburgh

If you're after a treat during your visit to Edinburgh, you'll find an increasing number of places which open the door to a bit of lavishness. Indulge in a cup of the world's best hot chocolate or dine from the kitchen of a Michelin-starred chef; float away from your troubles at a top-ranked spa; or take advantage of one of Edinburgh's luxury places to stay, which include a romantic castle and an OTT Gothic apartment in the heart of the Old Town.

▼ Witchery apartments

These unique themed rooms are a riot of indulgent baroque decor and escapist pampering.

P.160 ▶ ACCOMMODATION

▼ Restaurant Martin Wishart

Intricate French culinary techniques brought to bear on top-notch Scottish produce.

P.134 ▶ LEITH

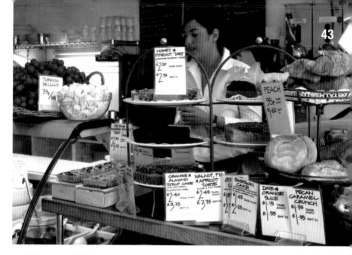

▲ Glass and Thompson

A classy sandwich or fresh pastry here is an essential part of any New Town exploration.

P.110 ▸ NEW TOWN

▼ Dalhousie Castle

A 700-year old castle on the outskirts of Edinburgh, beautifully converted into a luxurious country house hotel and spa.

P.165 ▸ ACCOMMODATION

▲ One Spa, Sheraton Grand

This superb ultra-modern hotel spa includes a range of revitalizing treatments, including a hydropool on the roof.

P.160 ▸ ACCOMMODATION

Festivals and events

Edinburgh likes to dub itself the "Festival City", but that doesn't just apply to August – at almost any time of year you'll find colourful events and celebrations which focus on different aspects of the city's history and cultural life. Some of these events link back to pagan ritual and are still celebrated with gusto – none more so than at the massive city-centre street party which marks Hogmanay, as New Year's Eve is known to Scots.

▲ Capital Christmas

Edinburgh's winter festival sees an outdoor skating rink installed in Princes Street Gardens.

P.181 ▸ ESSENTIALS

▲ Taste of Edinburgh

The city's best restaurants decamp to a tented village on the Meadows for a long weekend of noshing and nibbling.

P.180 ▸ ESSENTIALS

▲ Hogmanay

Edinburgh's massive New Year's Eve street party involves live bands, dancing, fireworks and 100,000 people singing *Auld Lang Syne*

P.181 ▶ ESSENTIALS

▶ Rugby Internationals

The atmosphere at top international games at Murrayfield can often be more significant than the result.

P.180 ▶ ESSENTIALS

▼ Beltane Fire Festival

Ancient Celtic celebrations marking the arrival of spring are re-created in a colourful night-time pageant on Calton Hill.

P.180 ▶ ESSENTIALS

Green places

Edinburgh's civic parks and protected green spaces are unique and incredibly varied. Central Edinburgh boasts rows of blossom-heavy trees and a beautifully manicured garden reclaimed from a stagnant loch, and there's also a lush 800-foot high peak within a mile of the centre, once part of the king's hunting ground. And if you feel like getting active, there are plenty of open spaces geared up for cycling, football or just sitting around.

▲ Holyrood Park

This spectacular sweep of heathery moor and craggy cliff includes the prominent peak of Arthur's Seat.

P.82 ▸ HOLYROOD AND ARTHUR'S SEAT

▼ The Meadows

With its cycle paths and open spaces, the Meadows are perfect for getting active.

P.143 ▸ SOUTH EDINBURGH

▷ Water of Leith

This verdant escape from the city centre links up a number of the sights worth seeing to the north of Edinburgh.

P.121 ▷ ALONG THE WATER OF LEITH

◁ Royal Botanic Garden

These seventy beautifully tended acres are perfect for lazy strolls.

P.121 ▷ ALONG THE WATER OF LEITH

▷ Princes Street Gardens

This wide swathe of lawn and mature trees makes a beautiful division between the Old and New towns.

P.100 ▷ ALONG PRINCES STREET

◁ Calton Hill

This distinctive landmark combines tall trees, grassy banks and wild gorse bushes as well as some off-beat architecture.

P.114 ▷ CALTON HILL AND BROUGHTON

Edinburgh views

Few European capitals offer so many different and dramatic vistas as hilly Edinburgh. It's a breathtaking city to explore on foot, with every steep climb rewarded with panoramic overviews across the rooftops to city landmarks, distant peaks and the shimmering Firth of Forth. And it's not just the topography that delivers – there are towers, bridges and even restaurants where you've little option but to stand (or sit) and stare.

▲ Salisbury Crags

The Radical Road footpath here offers a subtly changing overview of Holyrood and the new Parliament building.

P.82 ▸ HOLYROOD AND ARTHUR'S SEAT

▲ Oloroso

In good weather, the terrace of this swanky restaurant is *the* place to head for stunning scenic views over the chimneypots.

P.112 ▸ THE NEW TOWN

▲ Royal Botanic Garden

The panoramic views from the Botanics are dominated by the jagged Old Town skyline.

P.121 ▶ ALONG THE WATER OF LEITH

▶ Edinburgh Castle

From the castle's ancient ramparts you can enjoy a 360-degree outlook on the city – and any nearby invading armies.

P.63 ▶ THE ROYAL MILE

▼ Calton Hill

Whenever there's sunshine on Leith, you'll see it best from Calton Hill.

P.114 ▶ CALTON HILL AND BROUGHTON

Kids' Edinburgh

With spiral staircases and battlements to explore, "haunted" ruins full of beguiling nooks and crannies, Edinburgh has plenty to amuse young visitors. And while many of the major historic sites will undoubtedly appeal to kids' imagination, there are also lots of open spaces for running around as well as a number of excellent attractions specifically targeted at children – welcome respite if the city's emphasis on walking has worn out those younger legs.

▲ EICA:Ratho

This exciting new climbing centre has impressive facilities for kids, including a large soft play area and an exhilarating aerial assault course.

P.140 ▸ NORTH AND WEST EDINBURGH

▼ Edinburgh Zoo

Home of numerous rare and endangered animals, the zoo is a perennial kids' favourite.

P.136 ▸ NORTH AND WEST EDINBURGH

▲ Scottish Mining Museum

An unusual heritage museum in a converted colliery, where the tour includes a trip underground to the old coalface.

▼ Brass Rubbing Centre

Discover the timeless delights of brass rubbing in a converted church just off the Royal Mile.

◀ Our Dynamic Earth

Edinburgh's science centre uses a bit of hi-tech "time travel" to introduce the wonders of the natural world.

Modern architecture

For somewhere so famous for its rich history, much of it bound up in medieval buildings and Classical architecture, it's easy to overlook the dynamism of Edinburgh's contemporary offerings. Led by the eye-catching new parliament, innovative design is suddenly very much part of the Edinburgh picture, and there's a new-found appreciation of the contributions of modern architecture, both residential and in public buildings, to the already dramatic cityscape.

▲ Scottish Parliament

Enric Miralles' troubled yet thrilling design is a memorable tribute to his quirky approach, attention to detail and love of stylized imagery.

P.80 ▸ HOLYROOD AND ARTHUR'S SEAT

▼ Point Hotel

This converted department store is one of Edinburgh's most stylish places to stay, with interior decor at the cutting edge of contemporary design.

P.160 ▸ ACCOMMODATION

▲ Fishmarket Close

These new apartments in the heart of the Old Town are a highly successful modern interpretation of the area's traditional medieval tenements.

P.63 ▶ THE ROYAL MILE

▶ National Museum of Scotland

The custom-built museum is fascinating in itself, with labyrinthine corridors, oddly shaped rooms and occasional shafts of light and space.

P.88 ▶ SOUTH OF THE ROYAL MILE

◀ Dance Base

A brilliant example of how a modern structure, full of light and clever angles, can be fitted into a typically constricted Old Town space.

P.87 ▶ SOUTH OF THE ROYAL MILE

Shopping

Although the shops on Edinburgh's famous Princes Street can be a bit of a disappointment, you only have to shift a block away to George Street to find glamorous boutiques and upmarket emporia. Elsewhere in the city, it's often the smaller traders on the backstreets which capture the imagination: look out in particular for knitwear designers, antiquarian booksellers, jewellers and arts and crafts galleries.

▲ Victoria Street

The city's quaintest shopping street, with a string of unusual one-off shops that include a portmanteau maker and a cheesemonger.

P.87 ▸ SOUTH OF THE ROYAL MILE

▼ Anta

An appealing contemporary approach to tartans and tweed, specializing in bags, scarves, throws and fabrics.

P.92 ▸ SOUTH OF THE ROYAL MILE

▶ Ness

Fighting against the plethora of tacky souvenirs on the Royal Mile with some stylish and colourful contemporary clothing and accessories.

P.74 ▶ THE ROYAL MILE

◀ Jenners

The grande dame of Edinburgh shops, this old-fashioned department store has overseen the comings and goings of Princes Street for more than a century.

P.102 ▶ ALONG PRINCES STREET

▼ St Stephen Street

This intriguing Stockbridge sidestreet has a low-key collection of pubs, places to eat, secondhand clothes boutiques and craft shops.

P.123 ▶ ALONG THE WATER OF LEITH

▼ Harvey Nichols

The chic new kid on Edinburgh's shopping block, with four floors of all the most important designer labels.

P.110 ▶ THE NEW TOWN

Nautical Edinburgh

Edinburgh's former port, Leith retains an independent spirit born of cosmopolitan trade and seafaring connections as well as the need to reinvent now that shipping has changed entirely – the most prominent vessel docked here today is the former Royal Yacht *Britannia*, now a major tourist attraction. Edinburgh's other seaside suburbs – Newhaven and South Queensferry – offer an equally salty air, and you can even catch a glimpse of the sea right in the centre from Calton Hill's signal mast.

▼ Newhaven

A historic old stone harbour on the fringes of Leith where old boats bob on moorings alongside the city's fishmarket.

P.132 ▸ LEITH

▼ Nelson Monument

This oddly-shaped monument to England's most famous sailor is topped with an elevated viewing platform looking across Edinburgh and out to sea.

P.116 ▸ CALTON HILL AND BROUGHTON

▲ South Queensferry

This historic town perched on the shore of the Firth of Forth is the best place to take in the mighty Forth Bridges.

P.149 ▶ SOUTH QUEENSFERRY AND THE FORTH BRIDGES

◀ The Shore

Symbols of seafaring days abound along Leith's old harbour, now lined with pleasant pubs and places to eat.

P.131 ▶ LEITH

▼ Royal Yacht Britannia

Climb aboard to check that everything's as ship-shape as the flag locker, and as it was when *Britannia* was touring the world with the Royal family.

P.131 ▶ LEITH

Art outdoors

Edinburgh has a flourishing artistic tradition which is, inevitably, mostly celebrated indoors in the city's numerous art galleries. However, sculptors are among the artists most cherished by the city, and the compelling works of contemporary public art that are dotted all over the capital provide a quirky, unexpected antidote to the grand (if rather serious) architecture and impressive vistas which inevitably surround them.

▲ Landform

Charles Jenks' sinuous series of ponds and grassy mounds dominate the grounds of the Scottish National Gallery of Modern Art.

P.124 ▶ ALONG THE WATER OF LEITH

▶ Manuscript of Monte Cassino

Check out the distinctive pop art of local hero Eduardo Paolozzi in a pedestrian precinct near the top of Broughton Street.

P.117 ▶ CALTON HILL AND BROUGHTON

◀ Sculpture trail

The outdoor sculpture trail which leads through the grounds of the Scottish National Gallery of Modern Art and the neighbouring Dean Gallery includes works by Moore, Hepworth and Whiteread.

P.124 ▶ ALONG THE WATER OF LEITH

▲ Cone

Andy Goldsworthy's slate pine cone is one of a number of artworks dotted around Edinburgh's Botanic Garden.

P.123 ▶ ALONG THE WATER OF LEITH

▶ Pigeon sculptures

Shona Kinloch's bronze birdies scratch around on the pavement at Elm Row, near the top of Leith Walk.

P.114 ▶ CALTON HILL AND BROUGHTON

Places

GEOFFREY
KILTMAKER

TARTAN
for sale
BY
THE YARD

GEOFFREY KILTMAKERS

The Royal Mile

With its historic old buildings, closely packed tenements and shadowy closes, the Royal Mile ranks as one of the great streets of the world. Running downhill along a ridge from the cliff-skirted castle above the city to the Palace of Holyroodhouse, the Royal Mile remains medieval in character (if not always in reality), and is still the most resonant part of the Old Town, with a palpable sense that over the centuries most of Scottish history has passed this way. Even today it's at the heart of Scottish affairs, with politicians, judges and journalists mixing with the throngs of tourists ambling between the sights and souvenir shops.

Edinburgh Castle

Castlehill ☎ 0131/225 9846, ⊛ www .historic-scotland.gov.uk. Daily: April–Sept 9.30am–6pm; Oct–March 9.30am–5pm. £11.

Even given the wealth of Edinburgh's grand and historic sights, it's still the castle that defines the city. Perched on its high, impregnable crag of volcanic rock and protected by sheer cliffs on three sides, it has played a vital strategic role in Scottish affairs for hundreds of years. It was here that Mary, Queen of Scots, gave birth to her only child, James VI (the final king to use the citadel as a royal palace), and it last saw action in 1745, when Bonnie Prince Charlie's forces made a half-hearted attempt to storm it. The disparate styles of the fortifications reflect the change in its role from defensive citadel to national monument, and today, as well as attracting more visitors than anywhere else in the country, the castle is still a working military garrison as well as home to Scotland's crown jewels.

Though entry is fairly pricey, there's plenty to take

▼ EDINBURGH CASTLE

ROYAL MILE

LADY LAWSON STREET
WESTPORT
KING'S STABLES ROAD
JOHNSTON TERRACE
Edinburgh Castle
CASTLE ESPLANADE
CASTLEHILL
Ramsay Gardens
Witches Fountain
Scotch Whisky Experience
RAMSAY LA
Outlook Tower
Assembly Hall
The Hub
MILNE'S CT
GRASS MARKET
CANDLEMAKER ROW
COW GATE
GEORGE IV BRIDGE
Gladstone's Land
LAWNMARKET
Writers' Museum
JAMES CT
High Kirk of St Giles
Parliament House
BANK ST
Museum on the Mound
ST GILES ST
Heart of Midlothian
Parliament Square
Mercat Cross
WARRISTON'S CL
MARY KING'S CLOSE
ANCHOR CL
City Chambers
CHAMBERS STREET
FISH MARKET CL
Fringe Office
Cabaret Voltaire
STEVENLAW'S CLOSE
BLAIR ST
HUNTER SQ
Tron Kirk
COCKBURN ST
SOUTH BRIDGE
NORTH BRIDGE
Bannerman's
Honeycomb
NIDDRY ST
CARRUBER'S CLOSE
Whistlebinkies
N GRAY'S CL
Trinity Apse (Brass Rubbing Centre)
DRUMMOND STREET
INFIRMARY STREET
COWGATE
BLACKFRIARS ST
SOUTH GRAY'S CL
CHALMER'S CLOSE
JEFFREY ST
John Knox House/ Scottish Storytelling Centre
Museum of Childhood
ST MARY'S STREET
CRANSTON ST
EAST MARKET ST
Calton Old Burial Ground
PLEASANCE
NEW STREET
HOLYROOD ROAD
ST JOHN STREET
The People's Story (Canongate Tolbooth)
CANONGATE
Museum of Edinburgh
OLD TOLBOOTH WYND
Canongate Kirk
Scottish Poetry Library
CRICHTON'S CL
VIEWCRAIG STREET
DUMBIEDYKES ROAD
DUNBAR'S CLOSE
Dunbar's Close Garden
Calton New Burial Ground
REGENT ROAD
Scottish Parliament
QUEEN'S DRIVE
HORSE WYND
Queen's Gallery
ABBEY STRAND
ABBEYHILL CRESCENT
ABBEYHILL
Holyrood Park
QUEEN'S DRIVE
Palace of Holyroodhouse
Holyrood Abbey

Ross Bandstand
West Princes Street Gardens
THE MOUND
PRINCES STREET
East Princes Street Gardens
ROSE STREET
HILL STREET
GEORGE STREET
THISTLE STREET
FREDERICK STREET
HANOVER STREET
ST ANDREW SQUARE
Waverley Bridge
Waverley Train Station
NORTH BRIDGE
MARKET ST

0   200 yds

SHOPS

Cadenhead's Whisky Shop	i
Carson Clark Map Gallery	h
Coda	c
Corniche	f
Geoffrey (Tailor) Kiltmakers	e
Ness	a & d
Just Scottish	b
Ragamuffin	g

EATING & DRINKING

Always Sunday	7
Amber	1
Barioja	15
Black Bo's	12
Café Hub	3
Café Marlayne	6
Creelers	9
David Bann's	17
Deacon Brodie's Tavern	5
Jolly Judge	4
La Garrigue	13
North Bridge	10
Spoon	11
The Storytelling Café	14
The Tass	16
Wannaburger	8
The Witchery by the Castle	2

© Crown copyright

What's in a mile

The Royal Mile is, in fact, one mile 110 yards in length, measuring from the castle drawbridge to the gates of Holyroodhouse. "The Royal Mile" isn't an official postal address, however, and the street has different names at various points along its length. The short, narrow section from the castle to the roundabout outside The Hub is Castlehill; at this point it becomes the Lawnmarket; while east of the main junction with the Mound and George IV Bridge it is the High Street. The final section, after the junction with St Mary's Street, is the Canongate.

in, from dingy prisons to windy battlements. At the heart of the complex is Crown Square, where you'll find the Great Hall and the quietly reverential Scottish National War Memorial, as well as the Crown Room, where the nation's magnificent crown jewels are displayed beside the Stone of Destiny, a plain lump of masonry on which all kings of Scotland, since Kenneth MacAlpine in 893, have been crowned.

Elsewhere you'll find the interesting but not overly militaristic National War Museum of Scotland, smaller regimental museums and St Margaret's Chapel, the oldest surviving building in Edinburgh, constructed in the twelfth century by King David I as a memorial to his mother. The battlements in front of the chapel offer the best of all the castle's panoramic views, as well as a chance to look down the barrel of the fifteenth-century siege gun Mons Meg, which could launch a 500-pound cannonball nearly two miles. The castle's other famous cannon is the more modern piece of artillery which fires a single daily round (Mon–Sat) from Mills Mount Battery at one o'clock. Originally

designed for the benefit of ships in the Firth of Forth, the firing now provides a popular ceremony for visitors and a ritualized time signal for city-centre office workers.

Castle Esplanade

If you don't have the time or inclination to visit the castle itself, the Esplanade leading up to its drawbridge offers a taste of the precipitous location and eye-stretching views. Originally a parade ground, it serves as a coach park for much of the year these days, though between May and September huge temporary grandstands are erected for the Edinburgh Military Tattoo (see p.179), a shameless if spectacular pageant of swinging kilts and massed pipe bands which takes place during August. At the northeast corner of the esplanade, near the fairytale turrets and

▼ RAMSAY GARDENS AT NIGHT

Tours on (and under) the Royal Mile

It isn't hard to get a sense of history by strolling down the Royal Mile on your own, but if you really want to load up on facts and colourful anecdotes, sign up with one of the companies that offer guided historic walking tours here, including Mercat (℡0131/225 5445, ⓦwww.mercat-tours.co.uk) and Auld Reekie (℡0131/557 4700, ⓦwww.auldreekietours.co.uk). Both companies also offer a chance to explore the vaults and subterranean streets immediately under the Royal Mile; dark deeds and spooky stories abound on these expeditions, as they do on more explicit ghost tours conducted by the ghoulishly-dressed actors of the Witchery Tour (℡0131/225 6745, ⓦwww.witcherytours.com) and City of the Dead Tours (℡0131/225 9044, ⓦwww.blackhart.uk.com), who take groups on spine-tingling night-time graveyard visits. If you prefer your imagination to be roused in other ways, the Edinburgh Literary Pub Tour (℡0131/226 6665, ⓦwww.edinburghliterarypubtour.co.uk) mixes a convivial pub crawl with extracts from local authors acted out along the way.

The above tours cost in the region of £7–10 and most leave from the area opposite or outside the City Chambers, where the various companies have signboards set up.

odd angles of the Ramsay Gardens apartments, look out for the Witches' Fountain, an Art Nouveau plaque commemorating some three hundred women burned near the spot on charges of sorcery, the last of whom was put to death in 1722.

The Scotch Whisky Experience

354 Castlehill ℡0131/220 0441, ⓦwww.scotch-whisky-experience .co.uk. Daily: May–Sept 9.30am– 6.30pm. Oct–April 10am–6pm £9.25. This city-centre showcase for Scotland's national drink mimics the kind of tours offered at distilleries in the Highlands and Islands, and while it can't match the authenticity of the real thing, the centre does offer a thorough introduction to the "water of life" (*uisge beatha* in Gaelic). Tours start off with a dram (measure) of whisky, then move through a scale model of a distillery and an entertaining tutorial on the specialized art of blending, and conclude with a gimmicky ride in a moving

"barrel" car through a series of uninspiring historical tableaux. On the ground floor, a well-stocked shop gives an idea of the sheer range and diversity of the drink, while downstairs there's a pleasant whisky bar and restaurant, *Amber* (see p.75).

Outlook Tower

Castlehill ℡0131/226 3709, ⓦwww .camera-obscura.co.uk. Daily: April–Oct 9.30am–6pm; (July–Aug 7.30pm); Nov–March 10am–5pm. £7.50. Housed in the domed black-and-white turret atop the Outlook Tower, Edinburgh's camera obscura has been a tourist attraction since 1853, providing an intriguing bird's-eye view of a city going about its business. The "camera" consists of a small darkened room with a white wooden table onto which a periscope reflects live images of prominent buildings and folk walking on the streets below. In a world of webcams and hi-tech imagery, the camera obscura retains an appealing simplicity and nostalgic charm, though the

World of Illusions exhibition which occupies the other floors of the tower (included in the ticket price) does have a much more futuristic theme, displaying colourful holograms, 3-D pictures and other optical games with an obvious appeal to children of around six and upwards.

▲ THE HUB

The Hub

Castlehill ☎0131/473 2015, ⓦwww .thehub-edinburgh.com. Ticket office (ⓦwww.hubtickets.co.uk) Mon–Sat 10am–5pm (9am–7.30pm in Aug). Dominated by its towering black neo-Gothic spire, The Hub is the permanent headquarters of the Edinburgh International Festival (see p.177). The event itself takes place for three weeks each August and early September, but the Hub is open year-round, providing performance, rehearsal and exhibition spaces as well as a ticket centre and café. The building was constructed in 1845 as an Assembly Hall for the Church of Scotland; its 1999 conversion introduced some radically colourful interiors and art installations. On the ground floor is the vivid yellow and electric blue interior of *Café Hub* (see p.74); if it's not in use for a function, it's worth checking out the main hall upstairs, where the original woodwork and high-vaulted ceiling have been enlivened with a fabulous fabric design in Rastafarian colours, while on the main stairwell, 200 delightful foot-high sculptures depict Festival performers and audiences.

Gladstone's Land

477b Lawnmarket ☎0844/493 2120. Daily: April–June & Sept–Oct Mon–Sun 10am–5pm; July & Aug 10am–7pm. £5. This tall, narrow building – not unlike a canalside house in Amsterdam – is the Royal Mile's best surviving example of a typical seventeenth century tenement. While it's not the Old Town's raciest attraction, the half-dozen rooms on show do offer a palpable sense of home life in medieval Edinburgh. The building is owned by the National Trust for Scotland, who have carefully restored the rooms, filling them with period furnishings and fittings;

▲ NIGHT-TIME GHOST TOUR

in each a prim guide is on hand to answer questions and pass out a sheet detailing what's on show. The six stories of the "land" would have been home to various families living one on top of each other – the well-to-do Gledstanes, who built it in 1620, are thought to have occupied the third floor. The arcaded and wooden-fronted ground floor is home to a reconstructed cloth shop; pass through this and you encounter a warren of tight little staircases, tiny rooms, creaking floorboards and peek-hole windows. The finest room, on the first floor immediately above the arcade, has a marvellous painted ceiling, some fine old dark furniture and an array of attractive rugs and Dutch paintings. The upper floors contain apartments which are rented to visitors (see p.157).

Writers' Museum

Lady Stair's Close ℡0131/529 4901, ⓦwww.cac.org.uk. Mon–Sat 10am–5pm, plus Sun noon–5pm in Aug. Free. Tucked away in the charming Lady Stair's House – a Victorian embellishment of a seventeenth-century residence set to one side of an open courtyard – the Writers' Museum is dedicated to Scotland's three greatest literary lions, Sir Walter Scott, Robert Louis Stevenson and Robert Burns. Its slightly lacklustre collection includes portraits, manuscripts and showcases filled with odd knick-knacks and relics associated with the writers – Scott's walking stick and a plastercast of Burns' skull among them. Storyboards fill in the key details of the writers' lives and relationships with Edinburgh (Burns only ever made extended visits to the city), and there are also brief displays on Scotland's other notable authors. The house itself holds as much interest as the exhibits, its tight, winding stairs and poky, wood-panelled rooms offering a flavour of the medieval Old Town. Known as the Makars' Court after the Scots word for the "maker" of poetry or prose, the courtyard outside continues the literary theme with a series of paving stones inscribed with quotations from Scotland's most famous writers and poets.

Museum on the Mound

HBOS Headquarters, The Mound ℡0131/243 5464, ⓦwww .museumonthemound.com. Tues–Fri 10am–5pm, Sat & Sun 1–5pm. Free. Set inside the striking, Italianate headquarters of HBOS (Halifax Bank of Scotland) which sits prominently overlooking Princes Street Gardens on the Mound, this is quite a fun little museum all about money, with displays of unusual currencies from around the world, various fakes and forgeries and plenty about Scotland's central role in banking history.

Parliament Square

The central section of the Royal Mile is dominated by the High Kirk of St Giles, the centrepiece of the cobbled Parliament Square. Three sides of this area (it's no longer strictly a square) are taken up with the Neoclassical facades of the Law Courts, originally designed by Robert Adam but completed by Robert Reid; his elevated Ionic columns and Classical statuary are typical of Edinburgh's grand Georgian style, but in fact the location is really too cramped for such flourishes to work effectively. Hidden behind the facade is the much older Parliament House, built in the 1630s for the then separate Scottish Parliament. After the move to Westminster in 1707, Parliament House was incorporated into the law courts, and its main feature, the impressive 122-foot long main hall, today acts as a grandiose lobby for the courtrooms beyond. As the courts are open to the public, it's possible to get inside to look at the hall (Mon–Fri 9am–5pm; free), with its extravagant hammerbeam roof and delicately carved stone corbels. In the far corner a small exhibition details the history of the building and courts, but it's more fun simply to watch everyday business going on in the hall, with solicitors and bewigged advocates in hushed conferrals, often following the time-honoured tradition of pacing up and down to prevent their conversation being overheard.

Elsewhere in Parliament Square, not far from the entrance to St Giles, is the Heart of Midlothian, a pattern set in the cobblestones which marks the site of the demolished tollbooth and prison; locals used to spit on the door of the prison to ward off the evil contained therein, and some still carry on the tradition today.

High Kirk of St Giles

Parliament Square ☏0131/225 9442, ⓦwww.stgilescathedral.org.uk. Daily: May–Sept Mon–Fri 9am–7pm, Sat 9am–5pm, Sun 1–5pm; Oct–April Mon–Sat 9am–5pm, Sun 1–5pm. Free (photo permit £2). The original parish church of medieval Edinburgh, from where John Knox launched and directed the Scottish Reformation, St Giles is often referred to as a cathedral, although it has only been the seat of a bishop on two brief and unhappy occasions in the seventeenth century. Its location and historical significance mean that it is often used for high-profile religious services, such as when the Queen is in town or at the opening of Parliament, though in fact it is strictly still an ordinary parish church with a regular congregation. The resplendent crown spire of the kirk is formed from eight flying buttresses and dates back to 1485, while inside, the four massive piers supporting the tower were part of a Norman

PLACES The Royal Mile

▼ HIGH KIRK OF ST GILES

church built here around 1120. In the nineteenth century, St Giles was adorned with a whole series of funerary monuments on the model of London's Westminster Abbey; around the same time it acquired several attractive Pre-Raphaelite stained-glass windows designed by Edward Burne-Jones and William Morris. At the southeastern corner of the interior, the Thistle Chapel (£3 suggested donation) was built by Sir Robert Lorimer in 1911 as the private chapel of the sixteen Knights of the Thistle, the highest chivalric order in Scotland. The compact structure is an exquisite piece of craftsmanship, with huge drooping bosses and extravagantly ornate stalls showing off Lorimer's bold Arts and Crafts styling. A short service is held in the kirk every day (Mon–Sat) at noon with five services at various times on Sundays.

Mary King's Close

Warriston's Close ☎0870/243 0160, ⓦwww.realmarykingsclose.com. Daily: April–Oct 10am–9pm; Nov–March Sun–Fri 10am–4pm, Sat 10am–9pm; hour-long tours depart every 20min. £8.50. Running underneath the City Chambers (the home of Edinburgh's local government), Mary King's Close is one of the capital's most unusual attractions. When work on the chambers (initially designed to be a mercantile exchange) began in 1753, the existing tenements were only knocked down to the level of the High Street. Because the tenements had been built on a steep hillside, the lower parts of these houses, together with the old streets (or closes) which ran alongside them, were left intact but entirely enclosed among the basement and cellars of the City Chambers. You can visit this rather spooky subterranean "lost city" on tours led by costumed actors, who take you round the old, cold stone shells of the houses where various scenes from the Close's history have been recreated. As you'd expect blood, plague, pestilence and ghostly apparitions are to the fore, though there is an acknowledgement of the more prosaic side of medieval life in the archeological evidence of an urban cow byre. The tour ends with a stroll up the remarkably well-preserved Mary King's Close itself.

Brass Rubbing Centre

Trinity Apse Church, Chalmers Close, High St ☎0131/556 4364, ⓦwww .cac.org.uk. April–Sept Mon–Sat 10am–5pm, plus Sun noon–5pm in Aug. Free, though rubbings incur charges. Tucked down a close off the Royal Mile, Trinity Apse is part of the fifteenth-century Trinity Collegiate Church which was reassembled on this spot after the original was demolished in 1845 to

▼ BRASS RUBBING CENTRE

make way for Waverley railway station. Inside, a large variety of replica monumental brasses are available for making a rubbing, with the subject matter ranging from six-foot-tall medieval knights to swirling Pictish designs – all great fun for kids and adults alike.

Museum of Childhood

42 High St ☎0131/529 4142, ⓦwww.cac.org.uk. Mon–Sat 10am–5pm, plus Sun noon–5pm in Aug. Free. The Museum of Childhood has an odd history, having been founded in 1955 by a local councillor who heartily disliked children. In today's digital age the collection of dolls' houses, teddy bears, train sets and marionettes may be regarded as a little dull for some children, although their nostalgic charm often touches a chord with parents.

Scottish Storytelling Centre

43–45 High St ☎0131/556 9579, ⓦwww.scottishstorytellingcentre .co.uk. Mon–Sat 10am–6pm, plus Sun noon–6pm in July & Aug. Free. (John Knox House £3.50.) There are two distinct parts to this cultural centre: one half is a stylish contemporary development containing an excellent café (see p.75), the Netherbow Theatre and an airy Storytelling Court containing a small permanent exhibition about Scottish stories from ancient folk tales to Harry Potter. Conjoined to this is John Knox House, a fifteenth-century stone and timber building which is a classic representation of the Royal Mile in its medieval heyday with its distinctive external staircase, overhanging

▲ JOHN KNOX HOUSE

upper storeys and busy pantile roof. Inside, the house is all low doorways, creaking floors and ornate wooden panelling; it contains a series of displays about John Knox, the minister who led the Reformation in Scotland and established Calvinist Presbyterianism as the dominant religious force in the country. Famous for his preaching of a stern, hard-line Protestant creed, Knox was the author of a religious tract titled *The First Blast of the Trumpet Against the Monstrous Regiment of Women*, and during his time in Edinburgh he famously had run-ins with Mary, Queen of Scots, a Catholic.

Regular performances and events take place in the centre, particularly during the Festival.

The People's Story

Canongate Tolbooth, 163 Canongate ☎0131/529 4057, ⓦwww.cac.org .uk. Mon–Sat 10am–5pm, plus Sun noon–5pm in Aug. Free. With its turreted steeple and box clock overhanging the street, the late sixteenth-century Canongate Tolbooth is a distinctive landmark halfway along the Canongate. It's occupied by a local history museum, the People's Story, which contains a series of display cases, dense information boards and rather old-fashioned tableaux dedicated to the everyday life and work of Edinburgh's population down the centuries. This isn't one of Edinburgh's essential museums, but it does have a down-to-earth reality often missing from places dedicated to high culture or famous historical characters.

Museum of Edinburgh

Huntly House, 142 Canongate ☎0131/529 4143, ⓦwww.cac.org .uk. Mon–Sat 10am–5pm, plus Sun noon–5pm in Aug. Free. The city's principal collection devoted to local history, the Museum of Edinburgh is as interesting for the labyrinthine network of wood-panelled rooms within as for its rather quirky array of artefacts. These do, however, include a number of items of real historical significance, in particular the National Covenant, the petition for religious freedom drawn up on

a deerskin parchment in 1638, and the original plans for the layout of the New Town drawn by James Craig (see p.105), chosen by the city council after a competition in 1767.

Canongate Kirk

Canongate. Mon–Sat 10.30am– 4.30pm, depending on volunteer staff and church services. Free. Unrestricted access to grounds. Constructed in the 1680s to house the congregation expelled from Holyrood Abbey when the latter was commandeered by James VII, Canongate Kirk has a modesty rarely seen in churches built in later centuries, with a graceful curved facade, arched and round windows and a bow-shaped gable to the rear. The airy interior has an odd light blue colour scheme, as well as various crests and flags that highlight the kirk's continuing royal and military connections. An attractive and tranquil stretch of green in the heart of the Old Town, the surrounding churchyard affords fine views up to Calton Hill; it also happens to be one of the city's most exclusive cemeteries – well-known internees include the political economist Adam Smith, Mrs Agnes McLehose (one of Robert Burns' flames) and Robert Fergusson, regarded by some as Edinburgh's greatest poet, despite his death at the age of 24 – his headstone was donated by Burns, a fervent admirer. A statue of the young poet striding along the Royal Mile can be seen just outside the kirk's gates.

Dunbar's Close Garden

Dunbar's Close, Canongate. Unrestricted access. Free. A delightful discovery tucked in behind the high tenements of the Canongate,

▼ CANONGATE KIRK AND CEMETERY

▲ CARSON CLARK MAP GALLERY

Dunbar's Close Garden is a lovely little green oasis formally laid out with gravel paths, yew hedges, beds of lavender and grassy squares in the style of a seventeenth-century Old Town garden. It's not hard to imagine how peaceful a space like this would have been, a world away from the hubbub of the cramped, dirty, bustling medieval city – these days it's a perfect haven if you're foot-weary from the tourist trail or simply looking for a tranquil spot to read a book or nibble a sandwich. A board mounted on one of the old ivy-covered walls states the garden was donated to the city (somewhat bizarrely) by the Mushroom Trust of Edinburgh in 1978.

Scottish Poetry Library

5 Crichton's Close, Canongate ☎0131/557 2876, ⓦwww.spl.org .uk. Mon–Fri 11am–6pm, Sat 1–5pm. Free. Built in 1999, the Scottish Poetry Library is a small island of modern architectural and cultural eloquence amid a cacophony of modern building works, most prominently the new Scottish Parliament a few blocks away. The building incorporates a section of an old city wall, and the attractive contemporary design harmoniously incorporates brick, oak, glass, Caithness stone and blue ceramic tiles. The library contains Scotland's most comprehensive collection of native poetry, and visitors are free to read the books, periodicals and leaflets found on the shelves, or listen to recordings of poetry in English, Scots and Gaelic. Readings and events are organized throughout the year.

Shops

Cadenhead's Whisky Shop

172 Canongate ☎0131/556 5864, ⓦwww.wmcadenhead.com. Closed Sun. Founded in 1842, Cadenhead's looks fairly unassuming from the outside but stocks a vast range of spirits, with unique labels of gin and rum alongside a mind-boggling selection of independently bottled malt and blended whiskies.

Carson Clark Map Gallery

181–183 Canongate ☎0131/556 4710, ⓦwww.carsonclarkgallery.co.uk. Closed Sun. A wonderful emporium of antique maps, charts and globes which relate mainly, but not exclusively, to Scotland.

Coda

12 Bank St ☎0131/622 7246, ⓦwww .codamusic.co.uk. Just off the

▲ SHOPPING ON THE ROYAL MILE

Royal Mile on the way down the Mound, Coda specializes in CDs of contemporary Scottish folk and roots music.

Corniche

2–4 Jeffrey St ☎0131/556 3707, ⓦwww.corniche.org.uk. Closed Sun. Long before designer labels became currency of the high street, this tiny place was a treasure-trove of ladies' designer labels from Katherine Hamnett to Jean Paul Gaultier. There's also a menswear section.

Geoffrey (Tailor) Kiltmakers

57–59 High St ☎0131/557 0256, ⓦwww.geoffreykilts.co.uk. Probably the best of the Royal Mile's purveyors of kilts and associated paraphernalia, offering advice on getting kitted out in tartan and an outfit rental service. The shop is also famous for its "21st Century Kilts": designed as a fashion statement (with pockets for mobile phones) and made in materials such as leather, plain tweed and even camouflage.

Just Scottish

6 North Bank St, The Mound ☎0131/226 4806, ⓦwww .justscottishart.com. One of the better places hereabouts to hunt down decent quality mainstream Scottish crafts, with painting, sculpture, ceramics and jewellery

from some up-and-coming local artists.

Ness

336–340 Lawnmarket & 367 High St ☎0131/225 8815, ⓦwww.nessbypost.com. In the midst of dull woollen mill outlets, Ness sells a range of refreshingly upbeat, contemporary modern Scottish designer knitwear and accessories.

Ragamuffin

278 Canongate ☎0131/557 6007, ⓦwww.ragamuffinonline.co.uk. This vibrant, hippyish place selling designer knitwear and accessories in a burst of bright colours and groovy styles is an antidote to the beige V-neck sweaters piled high elsewhere on the Royal Mile.

Cafés

Always Sunday

170 High St ☎0131/622 0667. Proof that there's room for a bit of real food even on the tourist-thronged Royal Mile, this pleasantly positive independent café serves healthy lunches, homemade cakes, fresh smoothies and FairTrade coffee.

Café Hub

Lawnmarket ☎0131/473 2067. Radically coloured, well-run café in the Edinburgh Festival centre, with light modern meals served right through the day and most evenings, alongside teas, coffees, snacks and drinks. The large terrace is the best alfresco location on the Royal Mile.

Spoon

15 Blackfriars St ☎0131 556 6922. Down a side road off the High St, and a world away from

modern café blandness. The approach is simple, with short menus of imaginative soups, expertly crafted sandwiches and a daily special such as farmhouse cheddar tart or boudin noir salad. Good coffee and cakes, too.

The Storytelling Café

Scottish Storytelling Centre, 43 High St ☎0131 556 9579. Best café in a tourist attraction in this part of town, with a bright, modern and airy venue as well as a high standard of soups, snacks and light meals.

Restaurants

Amber

Scotch Whisky Experience, 354 Castlehill ☎0131/477 8477, ⓦwww .amber-restaurant.co.uk. Closed Sun & Mon evenings. A better eating spot than its tourist-strip location might suggest, serving a good choice of light food such as potted shrimp at lunchtime, and more substantial and expensive dishes in the evenings, when there's a "whisky sommelier" on hand to suggest the best drams to accompany your honey-roast rack of Highland lamb or saddle of Balmoral venison.

Barioja

19 Jeffrey St ☎0131/557 3622. Closed Sun except in Aug. Open right through the day and good for a lunchtime bocadillos sandwich or late-afternoon drink and snack, this Spanish-owned bar makes a decent stab at tapas in a metropolitan setting. Secure one of the few tables on the ground floor to get open views out to Calton Hill.

Café Marlayne

7 Old Fishmarket Close ☎0131/225 3838. Closed Sun & Mon in winter. A friendly French bistro located down a cobbled Old Town close. The food is freshly cooked and reasonably priced, though the odd shape of the restaurant means many tables feel a bit cramped.

Creelers

3 Hunter Square ☎0131/220 4447, ⓦwww.creelers.co.uk. Calm and pleasant seafood bistro featuring fish and shellfish caught and/or smoked by the owners from their base on the west-coast island of Arran.

David Bann's

56–58 St Mary's St ☎0131/556 5888, ⓦwww.davidbann.com. Thoroughly modern vegetarian restaurant, open long hours and offering a wide choice of interesting, unconventional dishes such as pistachio, sweet potato and chick-pea cakes or fennel and spinach tart. The prices are very reasonable and the overall design is stylish and classy – not an open-toed sandal in sight.

La Garrigue

31 Jeffrey St ☎0131/557 3032, ⓦwww.lagarrigue.co.uk. A place of genuine charm and quality, with a menu and wine list dedicated to the produce and traditions of the Languedoc region of France – the care and honesty of the cooking shines through in dishes such as cassoulet or bream with chard. Two courses at lunch are £13–15, rising to the £20-plus mark in the evening.

Wannaburger

217 High St ☎0131/225 8770, ⓦwww.wannaburger.com. A civilised but still slick local burger bar serving plump patties made with Scottish beef plus lots of additional fillings

▲ DEACON BRODIE'S TAVERN

including mozzarella and homemade guacamole. Also offers free-range chicken and decent bean burgers.

The Witchery by the Castle

352 Castlehill ☎0131/225 5613, ⓦwww.thewitchery.com. The restaurant that epitomises Edinburgh Old Town, with Gothic panelling, tapestries and heavy stonework all a broomstick-hop from the castle. The grand fish and game dishes are pricey, as is the wine, but you can steal a sense of it all with a pre- or post-theatre set menu (£12.95).

Pubs and bars

Black Bo's

57–61 Blackfriars St. Daily 4pm–1am. No soft sofas and no decent ales, but a good example of how to stay hip without going minimalist, with church pews and candles alongside original art and DJ decks. Just fifty yards from the Royal Mile, but well off the tourist trail.

Deacon Brodie's Tavern

435 Lawnmarket. Daily 10am–1am. A busy, slightly bland but landmark pub, named after the respectable late eighteenth-century town councillor who moonlighted as a burglar. He's said to epitomize the duality of Edinburgh's image as a dignified professional city with a shadowy underworld, and to have been the inspiration for Stevenson's *Dr Jekyll and Mr Hyde*.

Jolly Judge

7 James Court, Lawnmarket. Mon–Thurs 11am–11pm, Fri & Sat 11am–midnight. Venerable if slightly tatty low-ceilinged pub in an attractive courtyard off the Royal Mile. Cosy in winter, and pleasant outside in summer.

North Bridge

20 North Bridge. Sun–Thurs 11am–midnight, Fri & Sat 11–1am. Plush in-hotel cocktail bar, with its slick glass island bar contrasting with ornate pillars and original panelling. Brasserie-style food is served at intimate tables for two on the encircling balcony.

The Tass

1 High St. Mon–Wed 11am–midnight, Thurs–Sat 11–1am. A no-frills, no-pretensions traditional pub notable for regular folk music sessions and decent menu which includes items sourced from local butchers.

Holyrood and Arthur's Seat

Holyrood is home to three dramatically contrasting elements of Edinburgh: medieval history, in the royal palace of Holyroodhouse and its ruined thirteenth-century abbey; sensational modern architecture, in the form of Enric Miralles' dazzling but highly controversial new Scottish Parliament; and an invigorating blast of the great outdoors, in the cliffs and ridges of Edinburgh's most dramatic natural feature, the old royal hunting ground of Holyrood Park and its slumbering peak, Arthur's Seat. As a result, the area has an intensity and a sense of escapism which, when wrapped up together, can provide some slightly surreal moments, with groups of royalist tourists shuffling past a huddle of republican-minded politicians, or sharp-suited civil servants hurrying by cagoul-clad outdoor types setting out for Salisbury Crags.

Palace of Holyroodhouse

Main entrance from Horse Wynd
℡0131/556 5100, Ⓦwww.royal.gov
.uk. Daily: April–Oct 9.30am–6pm.
Nov–March 9.30am–4.30pm; £9.50 or
£13 joint ticket with the Queen's Gallery.
Holyrood became established as Edinburgh's main royal quarters during the reigns of James V and of his daughter Mary, Queen of Scots, who favoured it over the draughty castle. A century later Charles II's architects transformed it into one of the finest Scottish buildings of the age, but it wasn't until Queen Victoria's reign that a monarch travelled to Scotland frequently enough to establish an official residence. Visits by the Queen are common today (including regular trips in mid May and late June, when the

place is closed to the public), and are invariably surrounded by a great rousing of the nobility in Scotland as well as plenty of pomp and ceremony.

Compared to most royal palaces, visitor access to Holyroodhouse is extensive. A series of royal reception rooms feature some outstanding encrusted plasterwork, each more

▼ PALACE OF HOLYROODHOUSE

PLACES

Holyrood and Arthur's Seat

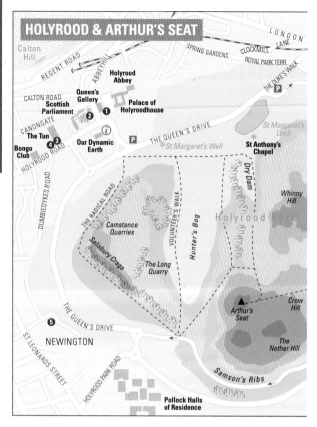

HOLYROOD & ARTHUR'S SEAT

impressive than the last – an idea
Charles II had picked up from
his cousin Louis XIV's Versailles
– while on the opposite side
of the internal quadrangle, the
Great Gallery extends almost

▼ PALACE TOWERS AND GATEPOST

the full length of the palace
and is dominated by portraits
of 96 Scottish kings, painted
by Jacob de Wet in 1684. It
was a ridiculous commission
by Charles II with laughable
results: the compliant De Wet
ensured that the Stewart family's
facial characteristics prevailed all
the way back to Fergus I. Just
beyond this, in the oldest part of
the palace, the formal, ceremonial
tone gives way to dark medieval
history, with a tight spiral
staircase leading to the chambers
used by Mary, Queen of Scots.
These contain various relics

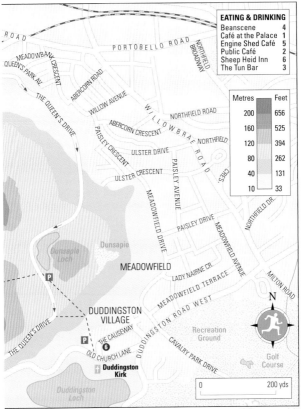

EATING & DRINKING

Beanscene	4
Café at the Palace	1
Engine Shed Café	5
Public Café	2
Sheep Heid Inn	6
The Tun Bar	3

Metres	Feet
200	656
160	525
120	394
80	262
40	131
10	33

© Crown copyright

associated with the queen, though the most compelling viewing is a tiny supper room, from where Mary's Italian secretary, David Rizzio, was dragged in 1566 by conspirators who included her jealous husband, Lord Darnley; a brass plaque in the outer chamber is said to mark bloodstains on the wooden floor where Rizzio was stabbed 56 times.

Holyrood Abbey

Access as part of Holyroodhouse tour (see p.77). Immediately adjacent to the palace are the poignant ruins of Holyrood Abbey, some of which date to the thirteenth century. Various invading armies paid little respect to the building over the years, and although it was patched up for Charles I's coronation in 1633 it was gutted in 1688 by an anti-Catholic mob. The roof finally tumbled down in 1768, but the melancholy scene has inspired artists down the years, among them Felix Mendelssohn, who in 1829 wrote "Everything is in ruins and mouldering . . . I believe I have found the beginning of my Scottish Symphony there today". Adjacent to the abbey are the formal palace gardens, open to visitors during the summer months and offering some pleasant short strolls.

Queen's Gallery

Horse Wynd ☎0131/556 5100, ⓦwww .royal.gov.uk. April–Oct 9.30am–6pm; Nov–March 9.30am–4.30pm. £5 or £13 joint ticket with Holyroodhouse.

Essentially an adjunct to Holyrood palace, the Queen's Gallery is located in the shell of a former church directly between the palace and the parliament. With just two principal viewing rooms, it's a compact space, but has an appealing contemporary style, which manages to remain sympathetic to the older elements of the building. It is used to display changing exhibitions from the Royal Collection, a vast array of art treasures held by the Queen on behalf of the British nation. Because the pieces are otherwise exhibited only during the limited openings of Buckingham and Windsor palaces, the exhibitions here tend to draw quite a lot of interest. Recent displays have included a priceless collection of drawings by Leonardo da Vinci and a glittering array of jewellery by Russian goldsmith Carl Fabergé.

The Scottish Parliament

Horse Wynd ☎0131/348 5000, ⓦwww.scottish.parliament.uk. Business days (normally Tues–Thurs) 9am–7pm; non-business days (normally Mon & Fri, or Mon–Fri if Parliament is in recess) 10am–6pm; Sat & Sun 10am–4pm. Free entrance to lobby and debating chamber; full guided tours £5.

By far the most controversial public building to be erected in Scotland since World War II, Scotland's unusual new parliament building is the home of the country's directly elected assembly, which was re-established in 1999 and looks after various domestic affairs devolved from the UK parliament at Westminster. Initial estimates for the building, constructed on the site of a disused brewery at the foot of the Royal Mile, were tentatively (and rashly) put at £40 million; the final bill in 2004 when parliament eventually moved in was over £400 million. The unique design is the vision of Catalan architect Enric Miralles, whose death in 2000 caused more than a few ripples of uncertainty as to whether the famously whimsical designer

▼ THE SCOTTISH PARLIAMENT

had in fact set down his final vision. There are six interlinked structures within the complex, among them Queensberry House, which dates back to 1681, and the rather more modernistic towers housing offices and committee rooms. Miralles had a

▲ OUR DYNAMIC EARTH

conviction that "the Parliament sits in the land", which helps explain the leaf or petal-shaped design of the central buildings as well as the grassy landscaping which leads off the shoulders of the parliament building to Holyrood Park. A number of motifs and odd shapes run through the design, including the anvil-like shape which clads the exterior of the building, and the extraordinary windows of the MSPs' offices, shaped like the profile of a mountain or a section of the Forth Rail Bridge and said to have been inspired by a monk's contemplative cell. The main debating chamber is grand yet intimate and undoubtedly contemporary, with light flooding in through high windows and a complex network of thick oak beams. The other part of the building freely open to the public is the entrance lobby; a small exhibition here provides some historical, political and architectural background to the parliament. However, for a better appreciation of the quality and detail of design, which seems to have been brought to every nook and cranny of the complex, it's well worth joining one of the hour-long guided tours which allow visitors a peek at the dramatic committee rooms with their

views of Salisbury Crags, the glass-roofed garden lobby and the modern Scottish art works which pepper the corridors.

Our Dynamic Earth

Holyrood Rd ☎ 0131/550 7800, ⓦ www.dynamicearth.co.uk. April–June, Sept–Oct daily 10am–5pm; July–Aug daily 10am–6pm; Nov–March Wed–Sun 10am–5pm. £8.95.
Laid out beneath a pincushion of white metal struts, this modern, hi-tech attraction based on the wonders of the natural world is principally aimed at families with kids between five and fifteen. Inside, a "time machine" elevator whisks you off to the creation of the universe, fifteen billion years ago, which is described using impressive wide-screen video graphics, eerie music and a deep-throated commentary. Subsequent galleries cover the formation of the earth and continents with crashing sound effects and a shaking floor, while the calmer grandeur of glaciers and oceans is explored through magnificent large-screen landscape footage. The "Casualties and Survivors" gallery illustrates the history of life on earth, from primordial swamps to life-size models of some of the odd creatures who once inhabited the earth; further on, the polar regions – complete with a real iceberg – and tropical jungles are imaginatively

re-created, with interactive computer screens and special effects at every turn. Outside, the dramatic amphitheatre which incorporates the steps leading up to the main entrance serves as a great venue for outdoor theatre and music performances, most notably during the Festival.

Holyrood Park

Unrestricted access.

A large area of parkland and rough hillside immediately to the south of the palace and new parliament, the former royal hunting ground of Holyrood Park is one of Edinburgh's greatest assets, a 650-acre swathe of rock, hill and moor which brings a taste of Highland wildness into the centre of the city. While old photographs of the park show crops growing and sheep grazing, it's now most heavily used by walkers, joggers, cyclists and other outdoor enthusiasts. A single tarred road, the Queen's Drive, loops through the park, enabling many of its features to be seen by car – however, you need to get out and stroll around to appreciate it fully. Following Queen's Drive in a clockwise direction from the palace gates, you'll arrive at St Margaret's Loch, a nineteenth-century man-made pond, above

which stand the simple ruins of St Anthony's Chapel. From here, the road around the back of Arthur's Seat is one-way only for vehicular traffic, and ascends to Dunsapie Loch, tucked in below the summit. If you're on foot and feeling reasonably intrepid, you can tackle the various paths that criss-cross the park, though decent walking shoes, a waterproof and drinking water are recommended. You can pick up a map of suggested walks, as well as information on the geology and flora of the park, from the Holyrood Park Information Centre (normally manned Mon–Fri 10 am–3 pm) in Holyrood Lodge on Horse Wynd.

Salisbury Crags

Holyrood Park. Unrestricted access.

A curve of red cliffs stretching from above Holyrood Palace to the steep north side of Arthur's Seat, Salisbury Crags are the face of an angled dolerite sill of hard teschenite rock which once lay under the volcanic deposits that form most of the rest of the park. From his observations here in the late seventeenth century, James Hutton, widely regarded as the father of geology, was able to confirm his theories about the

▼ HOLYROOD PARK

true age of the earth and its features. A path, known as the Radical Road after the unemployed "radicals" given the task of building it in the 1820s, follows the base of the crags and is arguably a finer walk than the sharper climb to the top of Arthur's Seat. As the path rises the city gradually reveals itself, the lower perspective of the crags clearly showing the dominance of Castle Rock and the ridge down which the Royal Mile runs. Note that unauthorized rock climbing is not allowed on the crags, and that although there is a rough path along the top of the crags, any exploration here is dangerous, particularly in wet, windy or misty conditions. A better looped walk of about an hour's duration from Holyrood is to follow the "Volunteer's Walk" up the glen behind the Crags, then return along the Radical Road.

▲ ARTHUR'S SEAT

Arthur's Seat

Holyrood Park. Unrestricted access.

At 823 Metre above sea level, the summit of Arthur's Seat easily overreaches all of Edinburgh's numerous high points. Part of a volcano which last saw action 350 million years ago, its connections to the legendary Celtic king are fairly sketchy: the name is likely to be a corruption of the Gaelic *Ard-na-said*, or "height of arrows". The simplest and safest approach to the top from most points in Holyrood Park is to walk around the Queen's Drive to Dunsapie Loch, from where it's a further twenty-minute climb up grassy slopes to the rocky summit. On a clear day, the views incorporate the Lothians, the Borders, Fife, a few Highland peaks and, of course, Edinburgh laid out on all sides.

Duddingston Loch and Village

Holyrood Park's only natural stretch of water, Duddingston Loch occasionally freezes over in winter and is perhaps best known as the location for the famous portrait of "the skating minister", one of the best-loved paintings displayed at the National Gallery (see p.102). Today it operates as a bird sanctuary (free access) with swans, herons and grebes often seen around its reedy fringes. Perched above the loch, just outside the park boundary, Duddingston Kirk dates back in part to the twelfth century and lies at the heart of Duddingston Village, an unspoilt corner of the city with cobbled lanes, cute cottages and, inevitably, high price tags. The *Sheep Heid Inn* here (see p.84) is one of Edinburgh's oldest pubs and a great waypoint if you're exploring the park; out at the back of the pub there's a traditional skittle alley, still very much in working order.

Cafés

Beanscene

67 Holyrood Rd. www.beanscene
.com. Part of a Scottish mini-
chain of coffee lounges where
the emphasis is on creating
an easy-going, unhurried
environment. Tapas-like snacks
are available, the doors shut at
11pm nightly, and there's often
good music either on the sound
system or live on certain nights.

Café at the Palace

Holyrood Mews (enter via Queen's
Gallery entrance or Horse Wynd). Given
the dearth of decent eating places
in the Holyrood quarter, this is
a good option for lunch or a
coffee, serving sandwiches, salads
and hot daily specials, including
produce from Sandringham and
other royal estates. Sit inside in a
pleasant glasshouse-style area, or
outside in a garden space with
views of the Crags. You don't
need a ticket for the palace or
gallery to get in.

Engine Shed Café

19 St Leonard's Lane. Closed Sun.
A converted railway engine
workshop, now used by a
learning-disability charity to
house a bakery, tofu-making
workshop and a large, bright
first-floor café serving fresh,
filling and inexpensive lunches,
snacks and cakes.

Public Café

Main lobby, Scottish Parliament.
MSPs and their guests have
private restaurants within the
parliament building, but the
simple café off the public lobby
has "place of the people" feel
to it and does benefit from
subsidized prices – a cup of tea
here is half the price of a high
street café.

Pubs and bars

Sheep Heid Inn

43 The Causeway, Duddingston.
Mon–Wed & Sat–Sun 11am–11pm,
Thurs & Fri 11am–midnight.
One of Edinburgh's best-
known historic pubs, the
building has barely survived
various predictable makeovers,
but despite this it remains an
attractive spot. The place is
well managed and there's more
care taken over the food here
than in many other traditional
pubs.

The Tun Bar

Holyrood Rd. Mon–Sat 11am–11pm,
Sun noon–6pm. Located in the
ground floor of the angular,
all-glass Tun building, this is a
popular meeting
point for journalists
and politicians
who have been
prised out of the
parliament's in-
house canteens.
Standing room only
after work; at other
times you might
find a chocolate-
coloured sofa to
sink into.

▼ SHEEP HEID INN

South of the Royal Mile

The section of the Old Town immediately south of the Royal Mile operates, quite literally, on two levels. On the upper tier, the elevated viaducts of George IV Bridge and South Bridge connect the Royal Mile with the city's university precinct, where a youthful, student atmosphere intertwines with the cultural tone provided by Edinburgh's principal history museum. Below runs the Cowgate, overshadowed by the tall buildings on either side but busy with clubbers after dark; and the more open Grassmarket, a former execution site that's now home to closely packed pubs, restaurants and boutique shops.

National Library of Scotland

George IV Bridge ☎0131/623 3700, ⓦwww.nls.uk. Mon, Tues, Thurs & Fri 9.30am–8.30pm, Wed 10am–8.30pm, Sat 9.30am–1pm. Free.

A looming, windowless facade staring out blankly from the east side of George IV Bridge, the National Library's bare classicism is a little forbidding, though it's worth stepping back to admire the allegorical figures by Scottish sculptor Hew Lorimer which decorate the exterior. This is Scotland's largest library and one of the UK's copyright libraries (it holds a copy of every book published in the country), and you have to apply for a readers' ticket to gain access to the collection. However, the interesting, well-researched small exhibitions on the subject of books, printing and the written word (mounted in a side gallery on the ground floor) offer the chance of a peek inside the building.

Grassmarket

An open, partly cobbled area girdled by tall tenements, the Grassmarket was used as the city's cattle market from 1477 to 1911. Despite the height of many of the surrounding buildings, it offers an unexpected view up to the precipitous crags of the castle and, come springtime, it's sunny enough for cafés to put tables and chairs along the pavement. Such continental aspirations are a bit misleading, however, as the Grassmarket is best remembered

▼ NATIONAL LIBRARY OF SCOTLAND

SOUTH OF THE ROYAL MILE

© Crown copyright

EATING & DRINKING

Assembly	17
The Atrium	7
Black Medicine Coffee Company	13
blue	7
Blue Blazer	18
Bow Bar	4
Brass Monkey	10
Café DeLos	12
Dragonfly	16
Elephant House	11
Favorit	19
Khushi's	1
The Grain Store	3
The Last Drop Tavern	5
Maison Bleue	2
The Outsider	9
Petit Paris	8
Suruchi	14
The Tower	15
Traverse Bar Café	7
Villager	6

SHOPS

Anta	b
Blackwell's	d
Fabhatrix	f
Farmers' Market	c
Godiva	g
Iain Mellis	a
Cheesemonger	
McAlister Matheson Music	i
National Museum of Scotland Shop	h
Wm. Armstrong	e

as the location of Edinburgh's public gallows – the spot is marked by a tiny garden. It was also the scene of the city's best-known civic uprising in 1736, when the Captain of the Town Guard, John Porteous, was dragged from the Tolbooth and lynched by a mob upset that he had escaped punishment after ordering the Guard to shoot into a potentially restless execution crowd; nine citizens were killed. The notorious duo William Burke and William Hare had their lair in a now-vanished close just off the western end of the Grassmarket, and for a long time before its relatively recent gentrification there was a seamy edge to the place, with brothels, drinking dens and shelters for down-and-outs. Tucked away in the northwest corner is the award-winning modern architecture of **Dance Base** ☎0131/225 5525, Ⓦwww.dancebase.co.uk), Scotland's National Centre for Dance, where classes, workshops and shows are held. Elsewhere, the Grassmarket's row of history-themed pubs have become a focus for many of the stag and hen parties which descend on Edinburgh, and there's also a series of interesting shops, in particular the string of offbeat, independent boutiques on Victoria Street.

Greyfriars Kirk and Kirkyard

Candlemaker Row ☎0131/226 5429, Ⓦwww.greyfriarskirk.com.
Entered by a gateway beside *Greyfriars Bobby Bar*, Greyfriars Kirkyard has a fine collection of seventeenth-century gravestones and mausoleums, including one to the Adam family of architects. The kirkyard is visited regularly by ghost tours (see p.66) and was known for grave-robbing

▲ GREYFRIARS KIRK

long before Burke and Hare became the city's most notorious exponents of the crime. Bizarrely, as recently as 2004 two youths were tried at the High Court under the ancient laws of "desecration of a sepulchre", after they broke into one of the mausoleums and were spotted playing with a skull. More significantly, the kirkyard was the setting, in 1638, for the signing of the National Covenant, a dramatic act of defiance by the Presbyterian Scots against the attempts of Charles I to impose an Episcopal form of worship on the country. In an undemocratic age, thousands of townsfolk as well as important nobles signed the original at Greyfriars; copies were then made and sent around the country with some 300,000 names being added.

Greyfriars Kirk itself was built in 1620 on land which had belonged to a Franciscan convent, though little of the original late-Gothic style building remains. A fire in the mid-nineteenth century led to significant rebuilding and the installation of the first organ in a Presbyterian church in Scotland; today's magnificent instrument, by Peter Collins, arrived in 1990.

Greyfriars Bobby Statue

George IV Bridge. For all Greyfriars' rich history, the kirkyard's international renown stems mostly from a scruffy wee Skye terrier, Bobby, who was owned by a police constable named John Gray. When Gray died in 1858, Bobby was found a few days later sitting on his grave, a vigil he maintained until his death fourteen years later. In the process, he became an Edinburgh celebrity, fed and cared for by locals who gave him a special collar to prevent him being impounded as a stray. A statue was modelled from life and erected soon after his death; it's located just outside the kirkyard opposite the pub bearing the dog's name. Bobby's legendary dedication easily lent itself to sentimental children's books and was eventually picked up by Disney, whose 1960 feature film hammed up the story and ensured that streams

of tourists have paid their respects ever since.

George Heriot's School

Lauriston Place ☎0131/229 7263, ⓦwww.george-heriots.com. The impressive four-turreted George Heriot's Hospital, often mistaken for Holyrood palace, is now one of Edinburgh's most prestigious fee-paying schools. Founded as a home for poor boys by "Jinglin' Geordie" Heriot, James VI's goldsmith, its array of towers, turrets, chimneys, carved doorways and traceried windows are one of the finest achievements of the seventeenth-century Scottish Renaissance. While you can't go inside, it's possible to enter the grounds during school holidays (via the gates on Lauriston Place) and take a stroll around the outside of the building and the interior quadrangle to admire the architectural finery from up close.

National Museum of Scotland

Chambers St ☎0131/247 4422, ⓦwww.nms.ac.uk. Mon–Sun 10am–5pm. Free. Scotland's premier museum incorporates two very different but individually iconic buildings. The honey-coloured sandstone Museum of Scotland building was custom-built in the 1990s, its modern lines and imaginatively designed interior offering a fresh – but still respectful – home for many of the nation's most important historical artefacts. The cylindrical entrance tower, with its echoes of Edinburgh Castle, has a doorway at its base which leads to the soaring central lobby, Hawthornden Court; from here, you can join one of the free guided tours on different themes that depart throughout

▼ LEWIS CHESSMEN IN THE NATIONAL MUSEUM

the day, or pick up an audio headset (also free) which provides detailed information on the displays. The collection tells the nation's history from earliest man to the present day and is generally, though not strictly, laid out in chronological order over seven different levels. The labyrinthine feel of the rooms and stairways is a little disorienting at first, though the unexpected views of different parts of the museum above and below are a deliberate effect by the architect to emphasize the interconnectedness of the layers of Scotland's history.

▲ INSIDE THE ROYAL MUSEUM

Some of the most precious artefacts are found in the galleries covering Scotland's earliest people on Level 0; these include the Trappain treasure hoard of silver plates, cutlery and goblets, and the Cramond Lioness, a sculpture from a Roman tombstone found recently in the Firth of Forth. Various contemporary artworks here, including pieces by Edinburgh-born sculptor Sir Eduardo Paolozzi and environmental artist Andy Goldsworthy, complement the historical items.

The scarcity of remains from the medieval period make levels 1 and 2 less cluttered than the upper floors, and both the Monymusk reliquary, an intricately decorated box said to have carried the remains of St Columba, and the delightful Lewis chessmen, exquisitely idiosyncratic twelfth-century pieces carved from walrus ivory, stand out in splendid isolation. The higher up you go, the more recent the history – the new

Modern Scotland gallery will open in 2008 on the top floor, Level 6 but for the moment you can explore the Sporting Scotland gallery and the Scottish Sports Hall of Fame. Highlights include Andy Murray's tennis racket and Graeme Obree's world-record-breaking "Old Faithful" bike, constructed using spare parts from a washing machine.

Above this is a small roof garden, accessed by a lift, which affords some great vistas of the city. Other fine views can be enjoyed from the museum's stylish *Tower* restaurant (see p.95).

Royal Museum of Scotland

Chambers St. Same hours as National Museum of Scotland. Free.

Next door to and interlinked with the Museum of Scotland (though with a separate entrance), the older part of the National Museum is a dignified Venetian-style palace from the 1860s. A wonderful example of Victorian Britain's fascination with antiquities and natural history, its exhibits are extraordinarily eclectic, from butterfly collections to colonial loot – ranging around the world and through many different aspects of science, history, design and nature. The wonderfully airy Great Hall, framed in cast-iron in the model of the Crystal Palace in London, holds sculptures from Classical Greece and Rome alongside Buddhas from Japan, a totem pole from British Columbia and the bizarre Millennium Clock, a ten-metre tall, Heath-Robinson-style contraption which clicks and whirls into motion at 11am, noon, 2pm and 4pm. Rooms leading off from here hold collections of stuffed animals and birds, though a number of the natural history galleries are under refurbishment in a major project which will last through to 2011. The more specialized collections on the upper floors

include Egyptian mummies, ceramics from ancient Greece to the present day, and a splendid selection of European decorative art.

Old College

South Bridge ⊕ www.ed.ac.uk.

The oldest remaining part of the University of Edinburgh, the Old College was founded as the "Tounis College" in 1583 by James VI; it's now Scotland's largest university, with nearly 20,000 full-time students and an expansive campus which covers much of the area between here and the north edge of the Meadows (see p.143). The original plan for the Old College came courtesy of Robert Adam, and work on his magnificent vaulted entrance of monolithic Roman Doric columns began in 1789. Adam's death in 1792 and the Napoleonic Wars halted progress, and the college was completed in 1816 in a considerably modified form by William Playfair, whose splendid 138 Metre-long Upper Library, now known as the Playfair Library, is one of the city's finest Neoclassical rooms. Housing offices and the law faculty, The Old College is still a working part of the university, though as a spectacle it suffers from the fact that the traffic and houses of South Bridge close in too much to allow you a proper perspective of Adam's façade. For a fuller sense of the building, wander into the internal quadrangle; it's also sometimes possible for visitors to have a look around

▼ OLD COLLEGE DOME

Burke and Hare

The story of Burke and Hare ranks as the most notorious of the dark deeds associated with Edinburgh's Old Town. In the early 1800s the anatomy classes at Edinburgh's medical school were constantly seeking bodies for dissection, which meant good business for bodysnatchers who would illegally dig up freshly interred corpses from the city's graveyards. Two Irish immigrants to the city, William Burke and William Hare, took to simply murdering travellers, waifs and strays – people no one would miss – and selling them to the school's anatomy professor. Their victims numbered into the teens before they were rumbled; Hare turned king's evidence and Burke was convicted of the murders. He was hanged in the High Street before a crowd of 25,000 and, inevitably, his body was given to the medical school for dissection.

the interior of the Playfair Library – ask at the reception on the ground floor (or phone ☎0131/650 8002).

Talbot Rice Art Gallery

Old College, South Bridge ☎0131/650 2210, ⊛www.trg.ed.ac.uk. Tues–Sat 10am–5pm, plus Sun 2pm–5pm in Aug only. Free. The small Talbot Rice Art Gallery displays, in rather lacklustre fashion, some of the University's large art and bronze collection, including a number of twentieth-century works by Scots Joan Eardley and William McTaggart. The main reason to head here, however, are the avant garde touring and temporary exhibitions which are mounted on a regular basis – the show held during the Festival is normally of a high standard.

Surgeons' Hall Museum

Surgeons' Hall, Nicolson St ☎0131/527 1649, ⊛www.rcsed.ac.uk. Mon–Fri noon–4pm; call or check website for details of extended summer opening hours. £5 adults, £3 concessions. This handsome Ionic temple built in 1832 by William Playfair as the home of Edinburgh's Royal College of Surgeons houses one of the city's most unusual and morbidly compelling museums. In the eighteenth and nineteenth

century Edinburgh developed as a leading centre for medical and anatomical research, nurturing world-famous pioneers such as James Young Simpson, founder of anaesthesia, and Joseph Lister, the father of modern surgery. The history of surgery takes up one part of the museum, with intriguing exhibits ranging from early surgical tools to a pocketbook covered with the leathered skin of bodysnatcher William Burke (see above). Another room has an array of gruesome instruments illustrating the history of dentistry; nearby is a small display dedicated to a past president of the college, Joseph Bell, whose diagnostic prowess was immortalized by one of his students, Arthur Conan Doyle, who based his famous detective Sherlock Holmes on Bell. The third and most remarkable part of the museum, the elegant Playfair Hall contains a bewildering array of specimens and jars from the college's anatomical and pathological collections dating back to the eighteenth century. A vital aid to teaching in those days, the rows of glass jars contain every conceivable body part in various states of repair, along with an equally stomach-churning but compelling array of bones, skeletons and graphic paintings

▲ MCEWAN HALL, EDINBURGH UNIVERSITY

illustrating war wounds from the Battle of Waterloo.

Shops

Anta

91–93 West Bow (Victoria St) ☎0131/225 4616, ⓦwww.anta.co.uk. Closed Sun. Three floors of Anta's distinctive designs, which offer an original contemporary adaptation of the tartan and tweed image – rugs, throws, curtains, bags and ceramics in muted but stylish tones and textures.

Blackwell's

53–62 South Bridge ☎0131/622 8222, ⓦwww.blackwell.co.uk. One of the city's larger bookshops, with a good range of titles relating to Edinburgh and Scotland. It's open on weekdays until 8pm, there's a *Caffè Nero* tacked on the side, and the numerous nooks, crannies and floors give it a cosy, quasi-academic feel.

Fabhatrix

13 Cowgatehead ☎0131/225 9222, ⓦwww.fabhatrix.com. A modern hat shop, at once funky and fashionable, with some seriously cool designs in felt or silk from £25. Good if there's a chilly wind blowing or you're going to Ascot.

Farmers' Market

Castle Terrace ☎0131/652 5940, ⓦwww.edinburghcc.com. Saturday 9am–2pm. Meat, fish, vegetables, fruit, cheese and bread, much of it organic, sold direct by farmers from around the Lothians, Fife and the Borders.

Godiva

9 Westport ☎0131/221 9212, ⓦwww .godivaboutique.co.uk. Combining contemporary pieces from fashion design students at the nearby College of Art with vintage finery, this is one of the city's most interesting independent boutiques.

Iain Mellis Cheesemonger

30a Victoria St ☎0131/226 6215, ⓦwww.ijmellischeesemonger.com. A cramped, pungent shop on colourful Victoria Street with rounds of British and Irish farmhouse cheeses piled alongside a perfectly matured selection from the Continent.

Edinburgh's theatreland

The small area under the western lee of Castle Rock, between the Grassmarket and Lothian Road, acts as a focus of Edinburgh's cultural life in the eleven months outside August's Festival. Here you'll find the circular Usher Hall, venue for major orchestral performances as well as middle-of-the-road rock and pop concerts; the Royal Lyceum Theatre, for mainstream theatre; the Traverse, one of Britain's leading venues for avant-garde theatre and new writing; and the Filmhouse, the city's principal arthouse cinema. For more on all of these venues, see Essentials, p.175.

McAlister Matheson Music

1 Grindlay St ☎0131/228 3827, ⊛www.mmmusic.co.uk. Closed Sun. The most pleasant and informed place to buy classical CDs in Edinburgh, with a decent selection of jazz and Scottish folk as well.

National Museum of Scotland Shop

National Museum of Scotland, Chambers St ☎0131/247 4422. One of Edinburgh's better showcases for quality modern Scottish crafts and jewellery, as well as tasteful gifts inspired by the museum's collection, and instructive children's toys and games.

Wm. Armstrong

83 Grassmarket ☎0131/220 5557, ⊛www.armstrongsvintage.co.uk. A wonderful emporium of secondhand clothing, from sixties floral dresses to brass-buttoned military jackets.

Cafés

Black Medicine Coffee Company

2 Nicolson Street ☎0131/557 6269. Just opposite the Old College, with chunky wooden furniture and the usual array of coffees, cakes and lunchtime platters.

Café DeLos

Royal Museum of Scotland, 2 Chambers St ☎0131/247 4111. The menu may not be startlingly imaginative, but the setting is a winner, right in the middle of the soaring, echoing atrium of the Royal Museum.

Elephant House

21 George IV Bridge ☎0131/220 5355, ⊛www.elephant-house.co.uk. Mon–Fri 8am–11pm, Sat–Sun 9am–11pm. Slated as one of the places where J.K. Rowling, then a hard-up single mum, nursed her cups of coffee while penning the first Harry Potter novel, this is a decent daytime and evening café with a terrific room at the back full of philosophizing students and visitors peering dreamily at the views of the castle.

Favorit

19–20 Teviot Place ☎0131/220 6880. Mon–Fri 8am–3am, Sat–Sun 10am–3am. Slick, modern café–diner in chrome and neon, dishing

▼ WM. ARMSTRONG DISPLAY

up coffees, fruit shakes and big sandwiches, as well as alcohol, right through to the wee small hours, making it a hit with the post-club crowd.

Restaurants

The Atrium

10 Cambridge St ☏ 0131/228 8882, ⓦ www.atriumrestaurant.co.uk. Closed Sat lunch and Sun. One of the most consistently impressive of Edinburgh's top-end restaurants. Quirky, arty design features include railway-sleeper tables, while the food focuses on high-quality Scottish produce, some of it sourced from the nearby farmers' market.

blue

10 Cambridge St ☏ 0131/221 1222, ⓦ www.bluebarcafe.com. Closed Sun. With minimalist modern decor, this impressive café/bistro hits the spot in terms of standards of food and service. It's handy for a quality pre- or post-theatre bite, with tasty modern dishes such as sea bass and tapenade or confit duck leg with champ for under £10, and is one of the city's more sophisticated child-friendly options.

The Grain Store

30 Victoria St ☏ 0131/225 7635, ⓦ www.grainstore-restaurant.co.uk. This unpretentious restaurant is a relaxing haven above the bustle of the Old Town, serving fairly uncomplicated but top-quality modern Scottish food such as saddle of venison with beetroot fondant or toasted goat's cheese with caramelized walnuts. Reasonable lunchtime and set-price options.

Khushi's

9 Victoria St ☏ 0131/220 0057, ⓦ www.khushis.com. The glitzy new premises may perhaps belie its status as one of the city's most venerable Punjabi institutions but *Khushi's* remains faithful to a long- standing ethos of serving peerless classics such as lamb bhuna and fish curries, all at extremely affordable prices. No alcohol served, though you can BYO or order one of the excellent lassis or soft drinks.

Maison Bleue

36–38 Victoria St ☏ 0131/226 1900, ⓦ www.maison-bleue.co.uk. A contemporary bistro with an eclectic menu of tapas-style food such as calamari, Merguez

▼ THE OUTSIDER

sausages or haggis balls in beer batter. The lunch and early evening menus are good value.

The Outsider

15–16 George IV Bridge ☎0131/226 3131. Style conscious, arty modern restaurant open right through from lunch to late evening and permanently filled with beautiful young things. The food, which leans towards fish, salads and healthier options, is fresh, modern, informal and, surprisingly, not overpriced.

Petit Paris

38–40 Grassmarket ☎0131/226 2442, ⒲www.petitparis-restaurant.co.uk. Closed Sun. Pleasingly realistic and moderately priced French bistro, coupling a sincere attitude with tasty Gallic nosh, including good plat du jour deals. The best dishes – slow-baked rabbit saddle, perhaps, or coq au vin à l'ancienne – are scribbled in indecipherable text on the blackboard, and there's outside seating.

Suruchi

14a Nicolson St ☎0131/556 6583, ⒲www.suruchiscotland.com. Popular establishment serving genuine South Indian dishes at moderate prices, though the menu is written in bizarre but entertaining broad Scots. Look out for cross-cultural specials such as tandoori trout.

The Tower

Museum of Scotland, Chambers St ☎0131/225 3003, ⒲www .tower-restaurant.com. Expensive but excellent modern Scottish food, such as shellfish and chargrilled Aberdeen Angus steaks, in a self-consciously chic setting on Level 5 of the National Museum of Scotland. At night you're escorted along

▲ PETIT PARIS DELIVERY VAN

the empty corridors to the restaurant, where spectacular views to the floodlit castle are revealed.

Pubs and bars

Assembly

41 Lothian St ☎0131/220 4288, ⒲www.assemblybar.co.uk. Daily 10am–1am. This hip hangout is a café-bar from breakfast through to mid-afternoon, then revs up in the evenings as a lively pre-club venue, with a roster of DJs through the week.

Blue Blazer

2 Spittal St ☎0131/229 5030. Daily 11am–1am, Sun noon–1am. This traditional Edinburgh pub with an oak-clad bar and church pews serves as good a selection of real ales as you'll find anywhere in the city.

Bow Bar

80 The West Bow (Victoria St) ☎0131/226 7667. Mon–Sat noon–11.30pm. Sun 12.30–11pm. Wonderful old wood-panelled

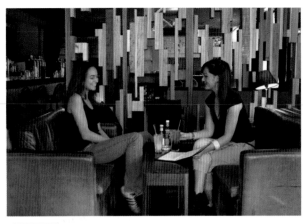

▲ ASSEMBLY BAR

bar that won an award as the best drinkers' pub in Britain a few years back. Choose from among nearly 150 whiskies, or a changing selection of first-rate Scottish and English cask beers.

Brass Monkey

14 Drummond St ☎0131/556 1961. Mon–Sat 11am–1am, Sun 12.30pm–1am. Comfortably straddles the fine line between style bar and boho hangout; it's slightly cramped in the main bar but the back room – which has a large lounge-styled cinema screen – comes complete with scatter cushions and Persian rugs.

Dragonfly

52 West Port ☎0131/228 4543, ⓦwww.dragonflycocktailbar.com. Fabulous service in funky surroundings where stylish cocktails are served up by even more stylish staff.

The Last Drop Tavern

74–78 Grassmarket ☎0131/225 4851. Mon–Sat 11am–1am. Sun 12.30pm–1am. The "Drop" refers to the Edinburgh gallows, which were located out front, and whose former presence is symbolized in the red paintwork of the exterior. Serves cheapish pub food and, like its competitors in the same block, enjoys the patronage of students and stag and hen parties.

Traverse Bar Café

Traverse Theatre, 10 Cambridge St ☎0131/228 5383. Mon–Wed 9.30am–midnight, Thurs–Sat 9.30am–1am. Closed Sun unless there is a show on. Much more than just a theatre bar, attracting a lively, sophisticated crowd who dispel any notion of a quiet interval drink. Good food, and snacks available after shows. One of *the* places to be during the Festival.

Villager

49–50 George IV Bridge. ☎0131/226 2781, ⓦwww.villager-e.com. Daily noon–1am. The bar of the moment in this part of town, so expect the local glitterati and lots of designer clothing in amongst the chocolate brown sofas and teetering bar stools.

Along Princes Street

Princes Street is very much the centre of Edinburgh, with trains pulling into Waverley Station, buses and taxis arriving from all points and the pavements thick with tourists and shoppers. The latter are found in their droves along the north side of the street, where chain stores and a hotchpotch of architectural styles create an unlovely prospect. This is immediately redeemed to the south via a swathe of gardens as well as monuments, grand galleries and an unforgettable vista of the castle and Old Town.

General Register House and New Register House

Princes St ☎ 0131/535 1314, ⓦ www .nas.gov.uk. Mon–Fri 9am–4.30pm. Free. With its dignified Corinthian pillars and dome, General Register House is the most distinguished building on Princes Street. It's best seen on the approach from North Bridge – the same perspective is hard to achieve closer up, which is why the streams of shoppers squeezing past routinely ignore it. It was designed in 1774 by Robert Adam as a custom-built home for Scotland's historic records, a function it has maintained ever since, today acting as the home for the National Archives of Scotland. Its elegant interior is centred on a glorious Roman rotunda, lavishly decorated with plasterwork and antique-style medallions. Visitors can look around the small exhibitions based on the archives which are mounted in the foyer, and while access to other parts of the building, including the rotunda, is normally restricted to those conducting historical research, staff may allow you in if you enquire at reception. Searches into family history are normally best begun at the adjacent New Register House. This is the home of the **General Register Office** for Scotland (ⓦ www .gro-scotland.gov.uk) and contains records of births, deaths and marriages. A dedicated Scottish Family History Centre, which will act as a single point of access for those researching genealogical records, is due to open within General Register House in 2008.

▼ PRINCES STREET AT NIGHT

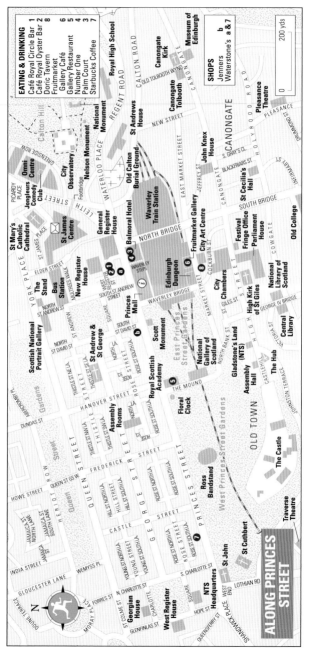

EATING & DRINKING
Café Royal Circle Bar 1
Café Royal Oyster Bar 2
Doric Tavern 8
Fruitmarket
Gallery Café 6
Gallery Restaurant 5
Number One 4
Palm Court 3
Starbucks Coffee 7

SHOPS
Jenners b
Waterstone's a & 7

0 ————— 200 yds

ALONG PRINCES STREET

© Crown copyright

Balmoral Hotel

1 Princes St ☎ 0131/556 2414, ⓦ www.thebalmoralhotel.com.

Dominating the east end of Princes Street, the *Balmoral* was built as a railway hotel in the early 1900s. For much of the century it was known as the *North British Hotel*, though by the 1980s the use of the imperial "North Britain" as an alternative name for Scotland didn't impress too many locals. The 188-room, five-star establishment is one of the grandest hotels in the city, though it maintains its close association with the railway: the timepiece on its chunky clocktower is always kept two minutes fast in order to encourage passengers to catch their trains at neighbouring Waverley Station, the city's principal mainline stop. Downstairs in the hotel is a Michelin-starred restaurant, *Number One* (see p.104); a meal in *Hadrian's Brasserie* or tea at the *Palm Court* is a more affordable way to get a taste of the place.

Edinburgh Dungeon

31 Market St ☎ 0131/240 1000, ⓦ www.thedungeons.com. April–June daily 10am–5pm; July–Aug daily 10am–7pm; Sept–Oct daily 10am–5pm. Nov–March Mon–Fri 11am–4pm, Sat & Sun 10.30am–4.30pm; £9.95.

An unashamedly OTT horror-themed attraction which aptly describes itself as "an orgy of grisly entertainment", the Dungeon is based in vaults beside the railway station. If you're tempted inside by the blood-spattered marketing, you'll encounter various scenes that use actors and gruesome special effects to ham up Edinburgh's associations with blood and gore of all varieties,

▲ BALMORAL HOTEL CLOCK

from sixteenth-century witchhunts to the bodysnatchers Burke and Hare. This isn't the place for historical authenticity, but it does do its best to scare the living daylights out of you.

Fruitmarket Gallery

45 Market St ☎ 0131/225 2383, ⓦ www.fruitmarket.co.uk. Mon–Sat 11am–6pm, Sun noon–5pm. Free.

Much altered from its days as the city's fruit and veg market, the stylish modern design of this dynamic and much-admired art space is complemented by the regular appearance of top-grade international artists – recent years have seen shows by the likes of Jeff Koons and Bill Viola. With exhibitions changing every couple of months, this is one of the city's best places to see contemporary art. Peter Fink's exterior light installation, which mimics the Northern Lights, gives the building some interesting hues after dark; there's also a pleasant café and good art bookshop inside.

City Art Centre

2 Market St ☎0131/529 3993,
ⓦwww.cac.org.uk. Mon–Sat
10am–5pm, Sun noon–5pm. Free.
This classic six-storey Old Town
building is used by the city
council to exhibit the best of
their own impressive collection
of Scottish art, as well as high-
profile touring exhibitions.
There's no permanent display,
and shows can range from
high-brow overviews of the
history of Scottish art to props
from *Star Wars*, but the larger
exhibitions are normally worth
checking out.

Princes Street Gardens

Princes St. Daily dawn–dusk. Free.
It's hard to imagine that the
gardens which flank nearly the
entire length of Princes Street
were once the stagnant, foul-
smelling Nor' Loch, into which
the effluent of the Old Town
flowed for centuries. Initially,
a canal was proposed to run
through the gardens; the railways
came along just in time to claim
the space, and today a sunken
cutting carries the main lines out
of Waverley Station to the west
and north. Once completed, the
gardens, split into East and West
sections, were the private domain
of Princes Street residents and
their well-placed acquaintances,
only becoming a public park in
1876. These days, the swathes of
green lawn, colourful flower beds
and mature trees are a green lung
for the city centre: local office
workers appear in their droves on
sunny days to take a picnic lunch,
while others use it as a traffic-
free short-cut. The gardens'
eastern section is home to an ice
rink (late Nov to early Jan daily
10am–10pm; £7) and a towering
Ferris wheel (same times; £2.50)
in the run-up to Christmas. The
larger and more verdant western
section holds a floral clock and
the Ross Bandstand, a popular
Festival venue.

Scott Monument

East Princes Street Gardens
☎0131/529 4068, ⓦwww.cac.org.uk.
Daily: April–Sept Mon–Sat 9am–6pm,
Sun 10am–6pm; Oct–March Mon–Sat
9am–3pm, Sun 10am–3pm. £3. The
most bizarre of Princes Street's
assorted sights, and the largest
memorial to a man of letters

▼ CITY ART CENTRE

anywhere in the world, the 200ft-high Scott Monument was erected in memory of prolific author and patriot Sir Walter Scott within a few years of his death in 1832. Regarded as the father of the modern novel, Scott was born in Edinburgh in 1771 and studied law at the university, gaining

▲ SCULPTURES IN THE NATIONAL GALLERY

fame initially for resurrecting old Scottish folklore and ballads. Though originally published anonymously, his famous *Waverley* novels made him a celebrity, and by the 1820s he was playing a central role in Scottish affairs, famously coordinating George IV's visit to Edinburgh and dressing the king up in tartan. The elaborate Gothic space rocket which commemorates Scott was designed by one George Meikle Kemp, a local carpenter and joiner; while it was still under construction, he stumbled into a canal one foggy evening and drowned. The architecture is closely modelled on Scott's beloved Melrose Abbey, while the rich sculptural decoration shows 64 characters from his novels. On the central plinth at the base of the monument is a statue of the writer with his deerhound Maida, carved from a thirty-ton block of Carrara marble. Inside the recently restored memorial, a tightly winding spiral staircase climbs to a narrow platform near the top: from here, you can enjoy some inspiring – if vertiginous – vistas of the city below and hills and firths beyond.

National Gallery of Scotland

The Mound ☎0131/624 6200, ⬤www .natgalscot.ac.uk. Daily 10am–5pm, plus Thurs till 7pm. Free, though some temporary exhibitions carry an entrance charge.

Scotland's national collection of international art centres on the two Neoclassical temples which sit alongside each other at the foot of the Mound. The original National Gallery building, furthest from Princes Street, was designed by William Playfair in the 1850s to echo but not mimic its earlier and more exuberant neighbour, the Royal Scottish Academy (see p.102). Both buildings have their own entrance facing Princes Street, though the main entry point to the complex as a whole is through the much newer Weston Link, built beneath the galleries looking out into East Princes Street Gardens. Contained within the National Gallery building is Scotland's premier collection of pre-twentieth-century European art, including a clutch of exquisite Old Masters and some superb Impressionist works. Though by no means as vast as national collections found elsewhere in Europe, the gallery benefits greatly from being a manageable size, its series of elegant octagonal rooms enlivened by imaginative displays and a pleasantly unrushed atmosphere. On the ground floor the rooms have been restored to their 1850s appearance with pictures hung closely together on claret-coloured walls, often on two levels, and intermingled with sculptures and *objets d'art* to produce a deliberately cluttered effect. As a result some lesser works, which would otherwise languish in the vaults, are displayed a good fifteen feet up. Though individual works are frequently rearranged, the layout is broadly chronological, starting in the upper rooms above the entrance, and continuing clockwise around the ground floor. Not all of the finest pieces are guaranteed to be on show, but it's worth looking out for highlights such as a superbly restored Botticelli, *The Virgin Adoring the Sleeping Christ Child*, as well as various important canvases by Titian and other Venetians, a poignant Rembrandt self-portrait, a rare early Vermeer, Antonio Canova's pure white marble sculpture of *The Three Graces*, and the excellent range of early, classic and post-Impressionist works, including some Degas bronzes and works by Gauguin, Van Gogh and Cézanne. Amongst the Scottish collection in the basement, there's a great introduction to the portraiture skills of Sir Henry Raeburn; his "skating minister" (which inspired Enric Miralles' designs for the new Scottish Parliament) is probably the gallery's best-loved piece.

Royal Scottish Academy
The Mound ☏ 0131/225 6671, ⓦ www.royalscottishacademy.org.

Daily 10am–5pm, Thurs till 7pm. Free. The elder and more extravagant of the two buildings which form the National Gallery of Scotland (see p.101) houses the Royal Scottish Academy, a private institution made up of the country's finest artists and architects. The annual RSA exhibition (April & May) is regarded as Scotland's pre-eminent show of work by living artists, while at other times of the year the twelve recently refurbished interior rooms over two levels are hung with major temporary exhibitions mounted by the National Gallery – recent highlights have been shows based on Monet and Titian. Designed by William Playfair in 1826 and extended by the same architect in 1836, the building displays a profusion of Neoclassical columns and detail, including a guard of sphinxes on the roof alongside a statue of Queen Victoria. The plaza outside is a popular spot for buskers, stalls and impromptu Fringe performances.

Shops

Jenners
48 Princes St ☏ 0131/225 2442. Edinburgh's oldest department store and often dubbed "the Harrods of the North", the venerable Jenners dates from the late nineteenth century and

The National Galleries of Scotland

The National Gallery of Scotland is just one part of the national art collection housed around Edinburgh. Elsewhere in the city the Scottish National Portrait Gallery (see p.105), the Scottish National Gallery of Modern Art (see p.124) and its neighbour, the Dean Gallery (see p.125) display other parts of the National Galleries' holdings. A free bus service (daily 10.45am– 5pm; every 45min) connects all four buildings.

▲ FRUITMARKET GALLERY CAFE

remains the retail experience of choice for Morningside ladies and New Town gentry. Still a few hints of *Are You Being Served?*, though under the ownership of the House of Fraser modern designer labels now set the tone.

Waterstone's

13–14 Princes St & 128 Princes St ☎0131/556 3034. As Edinburgh's independent booksellers have largely been squeezed out of business, it's the national chains which dominate. Waterstone's have two stores on Princes Street (as well as one on George Street); all give prominence to local guidebooks and Scottish writers, as well as hosting regular readings and events.

Cafés

Fruitmarket Gallery Café

Fruitmarket Gallery, 45 Market St ☎0131/226 1843, ⓦwww.fruitmarket .co.uk. This attractive café feels like an extension of the gallery space, its airy, reflective ambience enhanced by the wall of glass onto the street. Stop in for soups, coffees or a caesar salad.

Palm Court

Balmoral Hotel, 1 Princes St ☎0131/556 2414. A smart suite within the five-star *Balmoral*, where elevenses, pre-prandial nibbles or proper (though very expensive) afternoon teas with scones or egg-and-cress sandwiches are served to the melodic sounds of a harpist.

Starbucks Coffee

Waterstone's, 128 Princes St ☎0131/226 3610. One chain coffee shop worth mentioning, surrounded by books and with fantastic views across Princes Street Gardens to the castle.

Restaurants

Café Royal Oyster Bar

17a West Register St ☎0131/556 4124. An Edinburgh classic, with a splendidly ornate Victorian interior featuring stained-glass windows, marble floors and Doulton tiling. The expensive seafood dishes, including freshly caught oysters, are served in a civilized, chatty setting.

Doric Tavern

15–16 Market St ☎0131/225 1084, ⓦwww.thedoric.co.uk. Long-established, unpretentious bistro overlooking Waverley Station; the moderately priced food tends towards the predictable end of modern

▲ ALLAN RAMSAY STATUE, PRINCES STREET

Scottish cooking, with the likes of lamb cutlets served with onion marmalade, but it's a popular, easy-going spot with a pleasant wine bar alongside the dining room.

Gallery Restaurant

Weston Link, National Gallery Complex, Princes Street Gardens ☏0131/624 6580. Open for lunches and Fri/Sat eve. More refined lunchtime option to the clattering café in the new extension below the National Gallery, offering moderately priced modern dishes such as red mullet with saffron potato or Aberdeen Angus fillet with smoked garlic. Large glass windows and tiered seating offer views of Princes Street Gardens.

Number One

Balmoral Hotel, 1 Princes St ☏0131/557 6727, ⓦwww .thebalmoralhotel.com/restaurant1 .html. Chef Jeff Bland holds a Michelin star for his haute cuisine served in an overtly upmarket subterranean dining space. Lunches are (just about) affordable for a taste of the artistry; for a bravura performance there's a six-course tasting menu, with dishes such as foie gras poached in port, for £69.

Pubs and bars

Café Royal Circle Bar

19 West Register St ☏0131/556 1884. Mon–Wed 11am–11pm, Fri & Sat 11am–1am, Sun 12.30–10pm. As memorable as the *Oyster Bar* next door, the *Café Royal* is worth a visit just for its Victorian decor, notably the huge elliptical island bar and the tiled portraits of renowned inventors. More than that, the beer and food are good, too.

The New Town

From its outset, the New Town was planned as a total contrast to the Old Town: the layout was to be symmetrical, the streets broad and straight, and the architecture unashamedly grand and spacious. Though originally intended as a residential area, the central part of the New Town is now the bustling hub of the city's commercial and business life, dominated by shops, banks and offices. Its unique historic character, however, is obvious at every turn, especially if you head for the dignified Georgian streets to the north, which remain one of the best-planned, elegant quarters of any European city.

Scottish National Portrait Gallery

1 Queen St ☎ 0131/624 6200, ⊛ www .natgalscot.ac.uk. Daily 10am–5pm, plus Thurs till 7pm. Free, entrance charge for some temporary exhibitions.

A fantastic medieval Gothic palace in red sandstone, the Portrait Gallery makes an extravagant contrast to the New Town's prevailing Neoclassicism. The exterior of the building is encrusted with statues of famous national heroes, a theme reiterated in the stunning two–storey

▲ SCULPTURES ON DISPLAY AT THE NATIONAL PORTRAIT GALLERY

The design of the New Town

Various schemes for the expansion of Edinburgh to the land north of the Old Town were suggested through out the eighteenth century, but it wasn't until 1766 that a competition to design the New Town was held, and eventually won by 22-year-old local lad James Craig. His initial plan was based on the pattern of the Union Jack flag; the modified final version kept the Unionist street names but simplified the layout. The principal axis, George Street, was to run along the brow of the hill linking two elegant squares; parallel Queen Street and Princes Street would have houses on one side only, looking north to the Forth and south to the castle respectively. Interlinking streets were to run at right angles to the main thoroughfares, creating neat blocks of houses, with narrow lanes providing access for tradesmen and carriages. Once implemented, the design proved to be the finest example of classical town planning in Europe, the geometric pattern of streets subsequently copied not just in Glasgow during the nineteenth century, but also in many expanding North American cities such as New York and Chicago. The importance of Edinburgh's legacy was recognised in the 1990s when the New Town (in combination with the Old Town) was designated a World Heritage Site by UNESCO.

EATING & DRINKING

Café St Honoré	8	Iglu	4
Centotre	12	Mussel Inn	14
Cumberland Bar	1	Number 28	17
The Dome	11	Oloroso	16
Dusit	9	Oxford Bar	13
Fishers in the City	10	Queen Street Café	5
Forth Floor		Stac Polly	2
Restaurant	b	Tigerlily	15
Glass & Thompson	3	Valvona & Crolla	
Henderson's		VinCaffè	6
Salad Table	7		

THE NEW TOWN

N   0   200 yds

SHOPS

Joseph Bonnar	d
Cruise	f
Jane Davidson	c
Harvey Nichols	b
InHouse	a
Tiso	g
Waterstones	e

© Crown copyright

entrance hall by William Hole's tapestry-like frieze depicting notable figures from Scotland's past. Unlike the more global outlook of its sister National Galleries (see p.101), the portrait gallery devotes itself to images of famous Scots – a definition stretched to include anyone with the slightest connection to the country. Taken as a whole, it's an engaging procession through Scottish history, with familiar faces from Bonnie Prince Charlie and Mary, Queen of Scots, to Alex Ferguson and Sean Connery appearing along the way. The permanent collection is located on the two upper floors; though the paintings on display are changed frequently, there's normally a healthy representation of works by Scotland's best portraitists, from Allan Ramsay and Sir Henry Raeburn to contemporary luminaries such as David Mach and John Bellany. Temporary exhibitions are displayed in the galleries on the ground floor; elsewhere on this floor are the shop and café.

The Discovery Room

52 Queen St ☎ 0131/225 6028. Mon–Fri 9.15am–4.30pm. Free, but donation requested. This underplayed but highly significant spot is where Edinburgh doctor Sir James Young Simpson discovered the anaesthetic applications of chloroform, which revolutionized medicine in the mid-nineteenth century by providing the first

A short walk in the New Town

The colonization of Princes Street, George Street and Queen Street by shops and offices means that it can be hard to appreciate the elegant residential style which made the first phase of the New Town so attractive to Edinburgh's middle and upper classes in the late eighteenth century. Take a stroll down the hill to the later phases of the New Town and you'll find yourself in purely residential territory. Although many of the townhouses are now subdivided into flats, distinctive period features remain intact, including the fan-shaped windows above heavy doors with brass name plaques and handles, the stone detailing and tall, astragaled windows. Few streets fail to impress in what is, after all, a World Heritage Site, but to see some of the finest examples, walk the short circuit from Heriot Row, the street immediately north of Queen Street Gardens, through to Moray Place, along Doune Terrace and Gloucester Place then back up India Street.

effective form of pain relief in childbirth. The townhouse where Simpson lived and had his practice rooms is now run by the Church of Scotland as a drug counselling centre, but the old dining room where he made his first public demonstration of chloroform at a dinner party in 1847 has been left as a museum, with story-boards about Simpson's career and his experiments with different anaesthetics lining the walls. You may have to ring the door bell to get in, and though it's a little dowdy in appearance and inevitably of most appeal to those with an interest in medical history, the Discovery Room has an appealing simplicity and authenticity, and covers its subject as equally effectively as more glamorous history-themed museums.

Charlotte Square

Marking the western end of George Street, Charlotte Square is generally regarded as the epitome of the New Town's elegant simplicity. Designed by Robert Adam in 1791, it

immediately became the most exclusive residential address in Edinburgh, and though much of it is now occupied by offices, the imperious dignity of the architecture is still clear to see. Indeed, the north side, the finest of Adam's drawings, is once again the city's premier address, with the official residence of the First Minister of the Scottish Government at number 6 (Bute House), the Edinburgh

▼ CHARLOTTE SQUARE

equivalent of 10 Downing Street. In August each year, the gardens in the centre of the square are colonized by the temporary tents of the Edinburgh Book Festival (see p.178).

The Georgian House

7 Charlotte Square ☎ 0844/493 2118, ⓦ www.nts.org.uk. Daily: March & Nov–Dec 11am–3pm; April–June & Sept–Oct 10am–5pm; July & Aug 10am–7pm. £5. As the National Trust for Scotland's Gladstone's Land (see p.67) represents classic Old Town life, so their Georgian House provides a revealing sense of well-to-do New Town living in the early nineteenth century. Though a little stuffy and lifeless, the rooms are impressively decked out in period furniture – look for the working barrel organ which plays a selection of Scottish airs – and hung with fine paintings, including portraits by Ramsay and Raeburn, seventeenth-century Dutch cabinet pictures, and the beautiful *Marriage of the Virgin* by El Greco's teacher, the Italian miniaturist Giulio Clovio. In the basement are the original wine cellar, lined with roughly made bins, and a kitchen complete with an open fire for roasting and a separate oven for baking; video reconstructions of life below and above stairs are shown in a nearby room.

National Trust for Scotland Headquarters

28 Charlotte Square ☎ 0844/493 2100, ⓦ www.nts.org.uk. Mon–Sat 9.30am–5pm. Free. The NTS's love affair with Charlotte Square is continued on the south side, most of which is taken up with their headquarters. The buildings have been superbly restored over the past few years to something approaching their Georgian grandeur, and it's well worth taking a look at the sumptuous interior with its wooden panelling, intricate cornicing and large, bright rooms. On the first floor, a small gallery (Mon–Fri 11am–3pm; free) shows a collection of twentieth-century Scottish art, including a number of attractive examples of the work of the Scottish Colourists. Downstairs, there's a café (see p.110) and a shop selling National Trust books.

Dundas Street

A steeply inclined extension of Hanover Street, Dundas Street has a rich concentration of commercial art

▼ MORAY PLACE

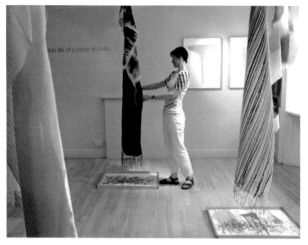

▲ DUNDAS STREET GALLERY

galleries which make for excellent browsing. While all are relatively small compared with Edinburgh's large public galleries, casual viewing is positively encouraged here and the work shown is almost always for sale, with prices ranging from a few hundred pounds for a limited-edition print to tens of thousands for work by the best-known contemporary artists from around the UK. Changing exhibitions give a different slant to each of the galleries listed here, though most places will show work by more than one artist at any given time. The very best of the bunch are right at the top of the street, by the corner of Abercromby Place. The dynamic Open Eye Gallery (Mon–Fri 10am–6pm, Sat 10am–4pm; ☎0131/557 1020, Ⓦwww.openeyegallery .co.uk) features exhibitions by Scotland's top contemporary artists. Other worthwhile stops nearby are Phoenix 369 at no. 3 (Tues–Sat noon–6pm, ☎0131/556 6497), which

majors in international contemporary work; the grander Bourne Fine Art at no. 6 (Mon–Fri 10am–6pm, Sat 11am–2pm; ☎0131/557 4050, Ⓦwww.bournefineart .com), which specializes in Scottish art from 1700–1950; and, at no. 16, the spacious Scottish Gallery (Mon–Fri 10am–6pm, Sat 10am–4pm; ☎0131/558 1200, Ⓦwww .scottish-gallery.co.uk), the oldest private gallery in Scotland, with a basement area dedicated to applied art. Further down are a number of smaller venues alongside antique and secondhand shops – the Torrance Gallery at no. 36 (Mon–Fri 11am–6pm, Sat 10.30am–4pm; ☎0131/556 6366, Ⓦwww.torrancegallery .co.uk), one of the first galleries in Edinburgh to specialize in contemporary art; and the Randolph Gallery at no. 39 (Mon–Fri 10.30am–6pm, Sat 10am–4pm; ☎0131/556 0808, Ⓦwww.randolphgallery.com), which tends to show a varied range of local art and crafts.

Shops

Joseph Bonnar

72 Thistle St ☎0131/226 2811.
Closed Sun. This wonderfully
old-fashioned shop, with its
dazzling range of antique gems
and trinkets, is one of the more
intriguing of Thistle Street's string
of small businesses and boutiques.

Cruise

80 George St ☎0131/226 3524. A
home-grown name which is
highly rated by Edinburgh's
fashionistas. The big George
Street branch has all the latest
in cool men's and women's
designer clothes.

Jane Davidson

52 Thistle St ☎0131/225 3280,
ⓦwww.janedavidson.com. Closed
Sun. A discreet frontage to three
floors of the hautest of couture
for women. Much loved by
Edinburgh ladies who find
department stores distasteful and
have access to a shimmering
credit card.

Harvey Nichols

30–34 St Andrew Square ☎0131/524
8388, ⓦwww.harveynichols.com.
Edinburgh's style cats were
greatly relieved when Harvey
Nicks finally arrived in town,
offering three floors of expensive
designer labels and an impressive
food hall and restaurant.

InHouse

28 Howe St ☎0131/225 2888,
ⓦwww.inhousenet.co.uk. Closed
Sun. Covetable contemporary
furniture, lighting and
kitchenware from designers
including Flos, Cassina and Alessi.

Tiso

123–125 Rose St ☎0131/225
9486, ⓦwww.tiso.com. Thurs till
7.30pm. The city centre's widest
selection of good-quality
outdoor gear, with waterproof
jackets, boots and camping and
sporting gadgets.

Cafés

Glass & Thompson

2 Dundas St ☎0131/557 0909.
Tasteful, upmarket café-deli
with huge bowls of olives and
an irresistible glass counter filled
with lovely food; scattered tables
and chairs mean you can linger
over a made-to-order sandwich
or top-notch cake and coffee.

Number 28

NTS Headquarters, 28 Charlotte
Square ☎0131/243 9339. Closed
Sun. Refined café authentically
decked out with severe
Georgian family portraits,

▼ HARVEY NICHOLS

▲ CAFÉ SAINT HONORÉ

serving porridge with cream for breakfast, classy light lunches and daytime tea and scones.

Queen Street Café

Scottish National Portrait Gallery, 1 Queen St ☎0131/557 2844. Tucked away from the main galleries, this self-service café enjoys a pleasantly unhurried atmosphere, and specializes in homemade soups, quiches and sweet treats.

Restaurants

Café Saint Honoré

34 North West Thistle St Lane ☎0131/226 2211, ⓦwww .cafesthonore.com.
A little piece of classical Paris discreetly tucked away in a New Town back lane. Fairly traditional French fare – grilled oysters, warm duck salad and tarte tatin – but top quality at moderate prices.

Centrotre

103 George St ☎0131/225 1550, ⓦwww.centotre.com. Slick and upbeat bar, café and restaurant in an ornate former bank, offering unfussy, top-quality Italian food from fresh pastries and coffee to interesting pizzas

or a simple but blissful plate of gorgonzola served with a ripe pear. All accompanied by a seriously impressive drinks list.

Dusit

49a Thistle St ☎0131/220 6846, ⓦwww.dusit.co.uk. The bold but effective blend of Thai flavours and well-sourced Scottish ingredients here brings a bit of originality and refinement to the often-predictable Thai dining scene. The moderately priced specialities include guinea fowl with red curry sauce or vegetables stir-fried with a dash of whisky.

Fishers in the City

58 Thistle St ☎0131/225 5109, ⓦwww.fishersbistros.co.uk. The New Town incarnation of Leith's best-loved seafood bistro has a sleek modern interior, great service and some top-notch (if expensive) seafood such as red snapper with samphire beurre blanc, or whole grilled lemon sole.

Forth Floor Restaurant

Harvey Nichols, 30–34 St Andrew Square ☎0131/524 8350, ⓦwww .harveynichols.com. Closed Sun & Mon evenings. Another Edinburgh restaurant with a view, and showing real confidence in its fine modern Scottish options – seared scallops with fig salsa, perhaps, or pot-roast pork. The expensive restaurant gets the glass frontage; the brasserie, with its simpler risottos and grills, is less pricey but set back from the views.

Henderson's Salad Table

94 Hanover St ☎ 0131/225 2131, ⓦ www.hendersonsofedinburgh .co.uk. Closed Sun. A much-loved Edinburgh institution, this self-service basement vegetarian restaurant offers freshly prepared hot dishes plus a decent choice of salads, soups and cakes. The slightly antiquated cafeteria feel can be off-putting, but the food is honest, reliable and always tasty. Light live jazz every evening.

Iglu

2b Jamaica St ☎ 0131/476 5333, ⓦ www.theiglu.com. A cosy contemporary bar with a small dining room upstairs which makes a decent fist of its self-declared status as an "ethical eatery" with well-cooked and presented dishes of organic, local and seasonal produce.

▼ WALL MOSAICS, MUSSEL INN

Mussel Inn

61–65 Rose St ☎ 0131/225 5979, ⓦ www.mussel-inn.com. After feasting on a kilo of mussels and a basket of chips for around £12, you'll realize why there's a demand to get in here. The owners include west-coast shellfish farmers, which ensures that the time from sea to stomach is minimal.

Oloroso

33 Castle St ☎ 0131/226 7614, ⓦ www.oloroso.co.uk. Edinburgh's most glamorous upmarket dining space, with a rooftop location giving views to the castle and the Forth. The expensive menu features strong flavours such as chump of lamb or halibut in a mussel and sorrel broth. Eating (or drinking) from the less intense bar is the cost-effective way to enjoy the setting, but the best views are from the balcony.

Stac Polly

29–33 Dublin St ☎ 0131/556 2231. Closed Sun & lunchtime Sat. Teetering on the edge of overbearing Scottishness, *Stac Polly* serves up local fare but avoids the kitsch with some classy touches, atmospheric surroundings and a hearty menu of game, fish and meat dishes.

Valvona & Crolla VinCaffè

11 Multrees Walk ☎ 0131/557 0088, ⓦ www.valvonacrolla .com. Suave, Milanese-style venue, which contrasts in style but not quality with the long-standing deli on Elm Row (see p.118). On ground level there's an espresso bar while upstairs you'll find dozens of top Italian wines by the glass, plates of antipasto and select mains.

▲ THE DOME

Pubs and bars

Cumberland Bar

1–3 Cumberland St ☎0131/558 3134. Mon–Sat 11am–1am, Sun 12.30–11pm. One of the few pubs in this part of the New Town, this mellow, cultured, old-fashioned place full of wood panelling and cosy nooks is a delightful find, and serves excellent cask-conditioned ales.

The Dome

14 George St ☎0131/624 8624. Mon–Sat 11am–1am, Sun 12.30–11pm. Opulent conversion of a massive George Street bank, thronging with well-dressed locals. Probably the most impressive bar interior in the city, with Grecian columns and a huge glass dome, while the stylish cocktail bar at the side is reminiscent of a 1920s cruise ship.

Oxford Bar

8 Young St ☎0131/226 2275. Mon–Sun noon–3am. An unpretentious, unspoilt, no-nonsense city bar – which is why local crime writer Ian Rankin and his Inspector Rebus like it so much. Fans duly make the pilgrimage, but fortunately not all the regulars have been scared off.

Tigerlily

125 George St ☎0131/225 5005. Daily 11am–1am. The epitome of George Street's transformation from the home of brogues and bowlers to a hang-out for bling and Boss. Multi-function venue (bar, restaurant, nightclub and boutique hotel) with extravagant interior decor and a startlingly high per capita consumption of pink champagne.

Calton Hill and Broughton

Edinburgh's longstanding tag as the "Athens of the North" is nowhere better earned than on Calton Hill, the volcanic crag which rises up above the eastern end of Princes Street. Numerous architects homed in on it as a showcase for their most ambitious and grandiose buildings and monuments, whose presence emphasize Calton's aloof air and sense of detachment today. But the hill and its odd collection of buildings aren't just for looking at: this is also one of the best viewpoints from which to appreciate the city as a whole, with its tightly knitted suburbs, landmark Old and New Town buildings and, beyond, the sea, which is much closer to Edinburgh than many visitors expect.

Calton Old Burial Ground

Waterloo Place. Open during daylight hours. Free.

Before the building of Waterloo Place and Regent Bridge (the elevated roadway which extends eastwards from Princes Street), Calton Hill was separated from both the Old and New Towns by steep-sided valleys. The hill

▼ ADAM SMITH MEMORIAL, CALTON OLD BURIAL GROUND

was formerly the site of a jail (demolished in the 1930s to make way for the looming Art Deco St Andrew's House, occupied by civil servants) and Calton Old graveyard, which survives today tucked in behind a line of high, dark, forbidding walls. The picturesque assembly of mausoleums and gravestones within, some at a jaunty angle and others weathered with age, make for an absorbing wander. Notable among the monuments is the cylindrical memorial by Robert Adam to the philosopher David Hume, one of Edinburgh's greatest sons, and a piercing obelisk commemorating various political martyrs.

Old Royal High School

Regent Rd. No public access.

With its bold central portico of Doric columns and graceful symmetrical colonnaded wings, Thomas Hamilton's elegant building of 1829 is regarded by many as the epitome

▲ OLD ROYAL HIGH SCHOOL

of Edinburgh's Athenian aspirations. The capital's high school was based here between 1829 and 1968, at which point the building was converted to house a debating chamber and became Scotland's parliament-in-waiting. However after the 1997 referendum, which came out in support of the re-establishment of a Scottish parliament, the building was controversially rejected as too small for the intended assembly, with a brand-new building at Holyrood favoured instead. Currently used as offices by the city council, the site has been earmarked for various suggested projects, which include a military heritage museum and museum of the history of photography, based around the work of 1840s photographic pioneers David Octavius Hill and Robert Adamson; the

EATING & DRINKING

The Barony Bar	2
The Basement	8
Blue Moon Café	4
Embo	1
Howies at Waterloo	10
No. 3 Royal Terrace	9
The Outhouse	6
Phuket Pavilion	5
Pivo	11
Planet Out	7
Rapido	3

SHOPS

Crombies	b
Joey D	c
McNaughtan's Bookshop	a
Valvona & Crolla	d
Villeneuve Wines	e

CALTON HILL & BROUGHTON

© Crown copyright

latter's studio, Rock House, was located on Calton Hill below the Observatory.

Ingleby Gallery

6 Carlton Terrace ☎0131/556 4441, ⓦwww.inglebygallery.com. Tues–Sat 10am–5pm. Opening hours may vary for certain exhibitions. Free. The loop of terraced streets which run around the eastern side of Calton Hill are among the finest examples of the New Town's Georgian grandeur. Most are still residential, although there are a number of diplomatic offices here, including the now heavily guarded USA Consulate. One typically elegant Edinburgh townhouse is occupied by the Ingleby Gallery, probably the most impressive small private art gallery in town, where you can view changing exhibitions by international contemporary artists including many of Scotland's premier stars such as Alison Watt, Craigie Aitchison and Callum Innes.

Nelson Monument

Calton Hill ☎0131/556 2716, ⓦwww .cac.org.uk. April–Sept Mon–Sat 10am–6pm, plus Sun noon-5pm during Aug; Oct–March Mon–Sat 10am–3pm. £3. Unusual in both its shape (an upside-down telescope) and theme (the victor at Trafalgar, generally regarded as one of England's, rather than Scotland's, great heroes), the Nelson Monument holds a prominent position at the top of Calton Hill. If you're feeling fit and want to upgrade Calton Hill's already impressive city views, you can climb the 143-step spiral staircase inside the monument; at the top, a viewing deck provides an interesting bird's–eye view of the odd assortment of buildings immediately alongside. Each day at 1pm, a white ball drops down a mast at the top of the monument; this, together with the one o'clock gun fired from the castle battlements (see p.65), once provided a daily check for the mariners of Leith, who needed accurate chronometers to ensure reliable navigation at sea.

National Monument

Calton Hill. Although it's often referred to as "Edinburgh's Disgrace", many locals admire this unfinished and somewhat ungainly attempt to replicate the Parthenon atop Calton Hill. Begun as a memorial to the dead of the Napoleonic Wars, a shortage of funds for the project led architect William Playfair to ensure that even with just twelve of the massive columns completed, the folly would still serve as a striking landmark. It's one of those constructions which is purposeless yet still magnetic; with a bit of effort and care you can climb up and around the monument, sit and stare for a while from one of the

▼ SHERLOCK HOLMES STATUE, PICARDY PLACE

huge steps or play hide-and-seek around the base of the mighty pillars. New schemes for the development of the National Monument and its Calton Hill neighbours, either grandiose or foolish (or both), are regularly proposed – one of these may some day be carried out.

City Observatory

Calton Hill. Designed by Playfair in 1818, the City Observatory is the largest of the buildings at the summit of Calton Hill. Because of pollution and the advent of street lighting, which impaired views of the stars, the observatory proper had to be relocated to Blackford Hill before the end of the nineteenth century, but the equipment here continues to be used by students. At one corner of the curtain walls is the castellated Observatory House, one of the few surviving buildings by James Craig, designer of the New Town. The complex isn't open to the public, but a stroll around its perimeter does offer a broad perspective over the city, with views out to the Forth Bridges and Fife.

Picardy Place

Between Calton Hill and the Broughton area, the large roundabout of Picardy Place links Leith Walk with the southeast corner of the New Town. It suffers from a high volume of traffic and a mess of conflicting architectural styles, in particular the brown concrete oblongs of the St James Centre, regularly cited as Edinburgh's greatest architectural blunder, and the new Omni Centre, which tries to make up for in plate glass what it lacks in grace. In amongst all these, however, are a few intriguing discoveries. At the foot of the steps in front of St Mary's Roman Catholic Cathedral is a wonderful three-part sculpture by Edinburgh-born Sir Eduardo Paolozzi. Titled *Manuscript of Monte Cassino*, it includes a giant hand holding a pair of tiny copulating grasshoppers and a robotic foot often employed by local toddlers as a makeshift slide. On the north side of the roundabout, set in front of a line of Georgian townhouses, is a statue of Sherlock Holmes who, though better associated with Baker Street in London, is commemorated here in tribute to his creator Sir Arthur Conan Doyle, who was born close by in 1869 and went on to study medicine at Edinburgh University, modelling his famous detective on one of his professors.

Broughton Street

Forming the eastern fringe of the New Town, Broughton Street is central Edinburgh's bohemian quarter, its string of bars, restaurants, food shops and arty boutiques making it a relaxed place to wander or hang out. It's also the centre of the city's gay scene, with a number of clubs, bars and gay-oriented organizations comfortably, rather than overtly, mixing into the general meld. While there aren't any mainstream tourist attractions hereabouts, the area does hold a few contemporary art galleries. The best of these are Edinburgh Printmakers at 23 Union St (Tues–Sat 10am–6pm; ☎0131/557 2479, ⓦwww .edinburgh-printmakers.co.uk), which has a studio and gallery dedicated to contemporary printmaking; and the small but sparse doggerfisher at 11 Gayfield Square (Tues–Fri

11am–6pm, Sat noon–5pm; ☏0131/558 7110, ⓦwww .doggerfisher.com), which shows avant-garde contemporary work in a converted tyre garage.

Mansfield Traquair Centre

15 Mansfield Place ⓦwww .mansfieldtraquair.org.uk. Normally open on the second Sun of every month, 1–4pm. During August the centre is used as an exhibition space. Check Fringe programme for details. Free. Built in neo-Norman style between 1872 and 1885 by Sir Robert Rowand Anderson for the Catholic Apostolic Church, the interior of this lovingly restored building is dominated by an outstanding scheme of mural decorations by Dublin-born Arts and Crafts artist Phoebe Anna Traquair. Covering vast areas of the walls and ceilings of the main nave and side chapels, the wonderfully luminous paintings depict

▼ TRAQUAIR MURALS, MANSFIELD PLACE CHURCH

Biblical parables and texts, with rows of angels, cherubs flecked with gold and worshipping figures painted in delicate pastel colours. The dilapidation of the church by the early 1990s prompted a campaign to save and protect the murals, which are now recognized as the city's finest in-situ art treasure.

Shops

Crombies

97–101 Broughton St ☏0131/557 0111, ⓦwww.sausages.co.uk. Closed Sun. Third-generation local butcher specializing in sausages, with over 100 different recipes: prune with cognac or basil, beef and blackberries alongside the more familiar Cumberland, Toulouse and chipolatas.

Joey D

54 Broughton St ☏0131/557 6672, ⓦwww.joey-d.co.uk. Don't mistake this tiny place for a fusty secondhand clothes shop – instead you'll find innovative recycled fashion wear for men and women, all designed and made on the premises.

McNaughton's Bookshop

3a–4a Haddington Place ☏0131/556 5897. Closed Sun & Mon. A fairly highbrow secondhand and antiquarian bookshop, with impressive sections on history, travel, art and Scottish classics.

Valvona & Crolla

19 Elm Row ☏0131/556 6066, ⓦwww.valvonacrolla.com. Arguably the finest Italian deli in Britain, with a van rolling in from Italy every week filled with the best possible produce. The floor-to-ceiling shelves are packed with wonderful cheeses, olive oils, salamis and wine, and a café at

▲ HOWIES AT WATERLOO

the back gives you the chance to indulge on the spot.

Villeneuve Wines

49a Broughton St ☎0131/558 8441, ⓦwww.villeneuvewines.com. Of Edinburgh's refreshing number of independent wine retailers, this has won crates of awards for their lively range of wines from small producers in both Old and New worlds. They also stock an impressive range of whiskies and Scottish beers.

Cafés

Blue Moon Café

1 Barony St ☎0131/556 2788, ⓦwww.bluemooncafe.co.uk. One of the best-known beacons of Edinburgh's gay scene, this easy-going, straight-friendly café-bar serves decent coffee, hearty breakfasts and moderately priced light meals right through to 11pm.

Embo

29 Haddington Place ☎0131/652 3800. Closed Sun. A cut above your average sandwich deli in quality (and price) this tiny but friendly place dishes out excellent fresh Mediterranean-influenced lunchtime food.

The distinctive chunky wooden tables and stools were constructed from Edinburgh trees struck down by Dutch Elm disease.

Restaurants

No. 3 Royal Terrace

3 Royal Terrace ☎0131/477 4747, ⓦwww.no3royalterrace.com. Pleasant if unadventurous mid-price dining on the ground floor of a grand Calton Hill townhouse – good for chargrilled steaks, fish and contemporary classics like Thai fishcakes or crème brûlée.

Howies at Waterloo

29 Waterloo Place ☎0131/556 5766, ⓦwww.howies.uk.com. Flagship of the Edinburgh-based mini-chain, with an elegant dining room close to Calton Hill's main sights and reliably well-priced, comforting modern Scottish food such as salmon with an orange and vanilla butter sauce, or pigeon with caramelized apple.

Phuket Pavilion

8 Union St ☎0131/556 4323, ⓦwww.phuket-pavilion.co.uk. Closed for lunch Sun. One of the more authentic

▲ PLANET OUT

Thai eating experiences in Edinburgh offering familiar yet colourful staples such as green curry, satay, and pad thai alongside a good range of specials.

Rapido

77–79 Broughton St ☎0131/556 2041. The best fish and chip shop in the area, and it even stays open after the pubs and clubs spill out. If you don't fancy the deep-fried fare there are pizzas, bruschetta and takeaway pasta options.

Pubs and bars

The Barony Bar

81–85 Broughton St ☎0131/557 0546. Mon–Thurs 11am–midnight, Fri–Sat 11am–1am, Sun 12.30–midnight. A fine old-fashioned bar which manages to be big and lively without being spoilt. Chainification has blunted a bit of its appeal, but there's still real ale and a blazing fire.

The Basement

10a–12a Broughton St ☎0131/557 0097. ⓦwww.thebasement.org.uk. Daily noon–1am, Sun 12.30pm–1am. This dimly lit, grungy drinking hole has long been a favourite of the Bohemian Broughton Street crowd, with odd furniture made from old JCBs and filling food served by Hawaiian-shirted staff.

The Outhouse

14 Broughton St Lane ☎0131/557 6668. ⓦwww.outhousebarbeque.com. Daily noon–1am. Busy pre-club bar tucked away down a cobbled lane off Broughton Street, with a lively beer garden and funky music.

Pivo

2–6 Calton Rd ☎0131/557 2925. Sun–Thurs 7pm–3am, Fri–Sat 5pm–3am. Decent small-hours drinking den with DJs every night and a pretty mellow clientele – the Czech theme begins and just about ends with the name.

Planet Out

6 Baxter's Place (Leith Walk) ☎0131/556 5551. Daily 4pm–1am. The liveliest of the local gay bars, this revs up fairly late, with DJs doing a pre-club routine.

Along the Water of Leith

Edinburgh's fairly placid Water of Leith is little more than a stream, but as it meanders through the city's northern suburbs, its course links various important sights, including the city's most dynamic art galleries, the tranquil Botanic Garden and the suburban villages of Dean and Stockbridge. Within walking distance of the city centre, and with a pleasant walkway running along the banks of the river, this stretch of the city makes a delightfully verdant escape from uptown's bustle and traffic, with both indoor and outdoor attractions, a good mixture of culture and nature, and a handful of attractive cafés, bars and restaurants.

Water of Leith Walkway

ⓦ www.waterofleith.org.uk.
Stretching thirteen miles along the entire length of the Water of Leith, this well-signposted walkway is easy to pick up along short sections where it runs through Edinburgh's northern suburbs, transporting you very quickly from the grand architecture of the New Town to a wooded gorge filled with the sounds of gurgling water and birdsong. The stretch heading west from Stockbridge past the Dean Village to the Dean Gallery is both a practical route between these spots, and a prettily varied walk through the deepest part of the gorge which passes a series of attractive old buildings, including St Bernard's Well, a Classical folly built over a mineral spring. In previous centuries the river was heavily polluted by the New Town's sewage and up to 100 different mills and small factories which were established along its length; today you might see a fisherman trying his luck on one of the slower stretches of the stream.

Royal Botanic Garden

Inverleith Row ☎0131/552 7171, ⓦ www.rbge.org.uk. Daily: Apr–Sep 10am–7pm, till 6pm March & Oct, till 4pm Nov–Feb. Free; £3.50 entry to glasshouses. Guided tours (April–Sept

▼ WATER OF LEITH WALKWAY PLAQUE.

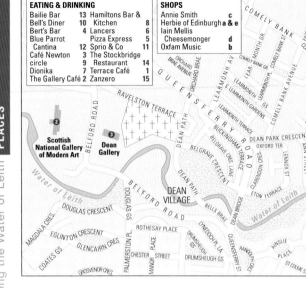

EATING & DRINKING		
Bailie Bar	13	Hamiltons Bar &
Bell's Diner	10	Kitchen 8
Bert's Bar	4	Lancers 6
Blue Parrot		Pizza Express 5
Cantina	12	Sprio & Co 11
Café Newton	3	The Stockbridge
circle	9	Restaurant 14
Dionika	7	Terrace Café 1
The Gallery Café	2	Zanzero 15

SHOPS	
Annie Smith	c
Herbie of Edinburgh	a & e
Iain Mellis	
Cheesemonger	d
Oxfam Music	b

11am & 2pm; 1.5hrs; £3) start at the West Gate on Arboretum Place.

Established on this seventy-acre site on the northern side of the Water of Leith in 1820, and

▼ ROYAL BOTANIC GARDEN

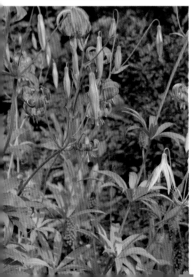

filled with mature trees and a huge variety of native and exotic plants and flowers, the "botanics" (as they're commonly called) are most popular simply as a place to stroll and lounge around on the grass. Towards the eastern side of the gardens, a series of ten glasshouses include the elegant 1850s Palm House, and a contrasting 1960s design with a complex exterior frame of struts and tensioners intended to maximise the amount of light and avoid the need for internal pillars. Inside, there's a steamy array of palms, ferns, orchids, cycads and aquatic plants, including some huge circular water lilies. Elsewhere in the garden, different themes are highlighted: the large Chinese-style garden, for example, has a bubbling waterfall and the world's biggest collection of Chinese wild plants outside China, while in

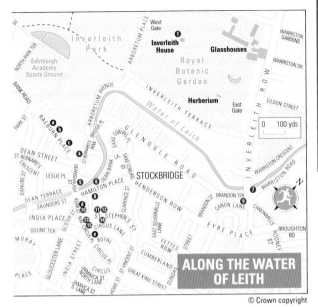

© Crown copyright

ALONG THE WATER
OF LEITH

the northwest corner there's a Scottish native woodland which very effectively evokes the wild unkemptness of parts of the Scottish Highlands and west coast. Art is also a strong theme within the botanics, with a gallery showing changing contemporary exhibitions within the attractive eighteenth-century Inverleith House at the centre of the gardens and, scattered all around, a number of outdoor sculptures, including a giant pine cone by landscape artist Andy Goldsworthy and the striking stainless-steel east gate, designed in the form of stylized rhododendrons. Parts of the garden are also notable for some great vistas: the busy *Terrace Café* (see p.127) beside Inverleith House offers one of the city's best views of the castle and Old Town's steeples and monuments.

Stockbridge

First established around the Water of Leith ford (and seventeenth century bridge) over which cattle were driven to market in Edinburgh, Stockbridge was essentially gobbled up in the expansion of the New Town, but a few charming buildings and an independent character prevail in the district today. It's a popular quarter for young professionals who can't afford the soaring property prices in the New Town proper, and as a result there's a good crop of bars, charity shops, vintage boutiques, delicatessens and places to eat along both Raeburn Place, the main road, and St Stephen's Street, long one of Edinburgh's more offbeat side-streets and a great place for some shopping or a bite to eat.

▲ STOCKBRIDGE

Dean Village

Less than half a mile upstream from Stockbridge the gorge of the Water of Leith becomes noticeably deep and steep. Nestled into the banks here, the old milling community of Dean Village is one of central Edinburgh's most picturesque – yet oddest – corners, its atmosphere of decay arrested by the conversion of numerous granaries and tall mill buildings into designer flats. More recent buildings have mimicked the style of the mills to maintain a sense of heritage and individuality, and the area makes a picturesque detour from the Water of Leith walkway. Surviving features of the Victorian community include the school, clocktower and communal drying green, while high above the Dean Village is Dean Bridge, a bravura feat of 1830s engineering by Thomas Telford, which carries the main road over 100 feet above the river.

Scottish National Gallery of Modern Art

75 Belford Rd ☎0131/624 6200, ⓦ www.natgalscot.ac.uk. Daily 10am–5pm, open till 6pm in Aug. Free. Accessed from the Water of Leith Walkway via a long, steep set of steps, the Scottish National Gallery of Modern Art was the first collection in Britain devoted solely to twentieth-century painting and sculpture. It operates in tandem with Dean Gallery across the road (see p.125); both galleries are located in impressive Neoclassical buildings which have been superbly converted into pleasant, relaxing viewing spaces, and both also have excellent cafés – if it's a sunny day head for the one at the Gallery of Modern Art, which has a verdant outdoor terrace. The extensive wooded grounds of both galleries serve as a sculpture park, featuring works by Jacob Epstein, Henry Moore, Barbara Hepworth and, most strikingly, Charles Jencks, whose prize-winning *Landform*,

▼ DEAN VILLAGE MILL AND THE WATER OF LEITH

Getting to the galleries

If you're heading directly to the Modern Art and Dean galleries from the city centre, you can jump on the free special bus service, which runs every 45 minutes (Mon–Sun 10.45am–5pm) from outside the National Gallery on the Mound, stopping at the National Portrait Gallery on the way. The only regular public transport running along Belford Road is bus #13, which leaves from the western end of George Street.

a swirling mix of ponds and grassy mounds, dominates the area in front of the Gallery of Modern Art. In contrast, there are few permanent works inside – one exception is Douglas Gordon's *List of Names (Random)*, an examination of "how our heads function", which lists in plain type on a white wall everyone the artist can remember meeting. Otherwise, the display space is divided between temporary exhibitions and selections from the gallery's own holdings; the latter are arranged thematically, but are almost constantly moved around. The collection starts with early twentieth century Post-Impressionists, then moves through the Fauves, German Expressionism, Cubism and Pop Art, with works by Lichtenstein and Warhol establishing a connection with the extensive holdings of Paolozzi's work in the Dean Gallery. There's a strong section on British artists, from Francis Bacon and Gilbert & George to Britart exponents such as Damien Hirst and Rachel Whiteread, while modern Scottish art ranges from the Colourists – whose works are attracting ever-growing posthumous critical acclaim – to the distinctive styles of contemporary Scots such as John Bellany, a portraitist of striking originality, and the poet-artist-gardener Ian Hamilton Finlay.

Dean Gallery

72 Belford Rd ☎0131/624 6200, ⓦwww.natgalscot.ac.uk. Daily 10am–5pm, open till 6pm in Aug. Free. The latest addition to the National Galleries of Scotland, the Dean is housed in a former orphanage which was dramatically refurbished specifically to make room for the work of Edinburgh-born sculptor Sir Eduardo Paolozzi, described by some as the father of Pop Art. The collection was partly assembled from a bequest by Gabrielle Keiller, and partly from a gift of the artist himself which included some 3000 sculptures, 2000 prints and drawings and 3000 books. There's an awesome introduction to Paolozzi's work by the huge *Vulcan*, a half-man, half-machine which squeezes into the Great Hall immediately opposite the main entrance – view it both from ground level and from the head-height balcony to appreciate the sheer scale of the piece. No less persuasive of Paolozzi's dynamic creative talents are the rooms to the right of the main entrance, where his London studio has been expertly recreated right down to the clutter of half-finished casts, toys and empty pots of glue. Hidden amongst this chaos is a large part of his bequest, with incomplete models piled four or five deep on the floor and designs stacked randomly on shelves. The ground floor also holds the

▲ PAOLOZZI'S STUDIO, DEAN GALLERY.

Roland Penrose Gallery's world-renowned collection of Dada and Surrealist art; Penrose was a close friend and patron of many of the movement's leading figures, and Marcel Duchamp, Max Ernst and Man Ray are all represented. Look out also for Dalí's *The Signal of Anguish* and Magritte's *Magic Mirror* along with work by Miró and Giacometti – all hung on crowded walls with an assortment of artefacts and ethnic souvenirs gathered by Penrose and his artist companions while travelling. The rooms upstairs are normally given over to special and touring exhibitions, which usually carry an entrance charge.

Shops

Iain Mellis Cheesemonger

6 Bakers Place ☎0131/225 6566, ⊛www.ijmellischeesemonger. com. Mon–Fri 9am–7pm, Sat 9am–6pm, Sun noon–5pm. Superb cave of farmhouse cheeses – the quality and range are

impeccable, and in foodie Stockbridge it's not unusual to see a queue out the door.

Annie Smith

20 Raeburn Place ☎0131/332 5749, ⊛www.anniesmith.co.uk. Closed Sun. One of a number of art and craft galleries in Stockbridge, with rings, bracelets and other minimalist silver jewellery handmade on the premises.

Herbie of Edinburgh

1 North West Circus Place & 66 Raeburn Place ☎0131 226 7212, ⊛www.herbieofedinburgh.co.uk. Closed Sun. Much-loved deli which has held its own by sourcing top-quality cheese, olives and wine. Best known for the wheel of ripe, gooey brie de meaux that sits on top of the display counter. Sit-down tables at the North West Circus Place venue only.

Oxfam Music

64 Raeburn Place ☎0131 332 7593. Daily 10am–5.30pm, Thurs open till 7.30pm. One of many charity shops in Stockbridge, this one specializes in old collectable vinyl, specialist music books, DVDs and CDs. The enthusiastic staff know their music and generally give good advice on what to buy plus local gigs worth checking out.

Cafés

Café Newton

Dean Gallery, 72 Belford Rd. Daily 10am–4.30pm. The more refined of the two cafés within the Dean and Modern Art galleries, with a high corniced ceiling and table service adding a touch of class. Filled focaccia as well as daily specials and excellent cakes are on offer.

circle

1 Brandon Terrace ☏0131/624 4666.
A pleasant café with lots of
local trade set in a cool room
of flagstone flooring and stone
walls. Serves a good choice
of patisserie and tray bakes,
sandwiches, light lunches, salads
or afternoon teas.

The Gallery Café

Scottish National Gallery of Modern
Art, 74 Belford Rd ☏0131/332 8600.
Daily 10am–4.30pm. Far more
than a standard refreshment
stop for gallery visitors, the
cultured setting (which includes
a lovely outside eating area)
and appealing menu of hearty
soups, healthy salads and filled
croissants pulls in reassuring
numbers of locals.

Sprio & Co

39 St Stephen's St ☏0131/226 7533.
Mon–Sat 8.45am–5.30pm, Sun
10am–5pm. Italian owned coffee
and sandwich bar with a good
dash of Milanese style and
swagger. Part of what makes
St Stephen's St so eclectic.

Terrace Café

Royal Botanic Garden
☏0131/552 0616. Daily
10am–6pm, closes 3.30pm
Nov–Feb. A great location
right in the middle of
the botanics, with outside
tables offering stunning
views of the city skyline.
Offers a decent array
of soups, snacks, daily
specials and coffees but
can be busy (and noisy)
with families.

Restaurants

Bell's Diner

7 St Stephen's St ☏0131/225
8116. Eves only, plus Sat
lunch. An unpretentious front-
room restaurant with a simple
mid-priced American menu
of home-made burgers, steaks,
milkshakes and pancakes. It's a
longstanding local favourite, so
tables aren't easy to come by.

Blue Parrot Cantina

49 St Stephen's St ☏0131/225
2941. Eves only, plus Sat lunch.
Cosy, quirky, moderately priced
basement Mexican restaurant,
with a frequently changing
evening menu that makes a
decent effort to deviate from
the predictable clichés via house
specialities such as *pescado baja*
(haddock with a creamy lime
sauce).

Dionika

3–6 Canonmills Bridge ☏0131/652
3993, ⌽www.dionika.com. Closed
Mon. Deli, restaurant and tapas
bar near the Botanic Garden,
with a strong Spanish accent;
the star turn is the seafood
paella.

▼ OUTDOOR CAFÉ, SCOTTISH NATIONAL GALLERY OF
MODERN ART

Lancers

5 Hamilton Place ☎0131/332 3444.
A reliable old-school Indian
restaurant serving mostly rich,
filling Bengali and Punjabi
curries at moderate prices.

Pizza Express

1 Deanhaugh St ☎0131/332 7229,
ⓦwww.pizzaexpress.co.uk. The
chain with the winning formula
for smart interiors and decent
pizzas comes up trumps with a
terrific location in a clocktower
building nuzzled right beside
the Water of Leith.

The Stockbridge Restaurant

54 St Stephen's St ☎0131/226 6766,
ⓦwww.thestockbridgerestaurant
.com. Closed Mon. Unusual but
endearing chef-run basement
venue that's established itself as
the best fine dining restaurant
in the district. Serves quite
grand modern Scottish dishes,
though there are some value

set price deals and even an
occasional "tot's taster menu".

Zanzero

14/16 North West Circus Place
☎0131/220 0333, ⓦwww.zanzero
.com. Up beat, spirited, youthful
café-bar-restaurant from the
owners of *Centotre* in the New
Town. Italian-oriented menu,
but the sight of a chianti bottle
in raffia would cause heart
failure. Lots of light, healthy,
lively food and wine.

Pubs and bars

Bailie Bar

2 St Stephen's St ☎0131/225 4673.
Sun–Thurs 12.30pm–midnight, Fri &
Sat 11am–1am. The best of the
district's traditional pubs, with
English and Scottish ales and a
good range of local characters.

Bert's Bar

2–4 Raeburn Place ☎0131/343 3000.
Mon–Thurs 11am–11pm, Fri & Sat
11am–midnight, Sun 12.30–11pm.
Popular locals' pub with a lived-
in feel. Serves excellent Scottish
ales, tasty pies and strives to
be an authentic, non-theme-
oriented venue, with 3 large
screen TVs rarely missing any
sporting action.

Hamilton's Bar & Kitchen

16–18 Hamilton Place ☎0131/226
4199, ⓦwww.hamiltonsbar
.co.uk. Mon–Sat 11am–1am, Sun
11am–midnight. One of the few
self-proclaimed gastropubs in
the city, where the food is of
equal importance to the booze.
Expect dark wood fittings and
sea bass with your chips.

▼ BAILIE BAR LAMP

Leith

Although Leith is generally known as the port of Edinburgh, it developed independently of the city up the hill, its history bound up in the hard graft of fishing, shipbuilding and trade. The presence of sailors, merchants and continental traders gave the place a cosmopolitan – if slightly rough – edge, which is still obvious today in Leith's fascinating mix of cobbled streets and flash new housing, container ships and historic buildings, ugly council flats and trendy waterside bistros. While the stand-alone attractions are few, Leith is an intriguing place to explore, worth visiting not just for the contrasts to central Edinburgh, but also for its nautical air and the excellent eating and drinking scene, which majors on seafood but also includes haute cuisine and well-worn, friendly pubs.

Leith Links

An area of predominantly flat parkland on the eastern side of Leith, the clue to Leith Links' place in history is (to golfers at least) in the name. Documentary evidence from 1505 suggests that James IV used to "play at gowf at Leithe", giving rise to Leith's claim as the birthplace of the sport. In 1744 the first written rules of golf were drawn up here by the Honourable Company of Edinburgh Golfers, ten years before they were formalized in St Andrews. Golf fans keen to pay homage to the spot may be a little disappointed, however: the only recognition given to this piece of sporting history is a commemorative cairn beside Duncan Place showing the layout of the original five-hole course, and

▼ THE SHORE, LEITH

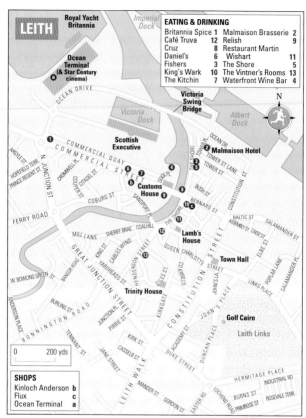

LEITH

Royal Yacht Britannia

Ocean Terminal (& Star Century cinema)

Imperial Dock

OCEAN DRIVE

Victoria Dock

Victoria Swing Bridge

Albert Dock

Scottish Executive

COMMERCIAL QUAY

COMMERCIAL STREET

Customs House

Malmaison Hotel

Lamb's House

Town Hall

Trinity House

Golf Cairn

Leith Links

N

EATING & DRINKING			
Britannia Spice	1	Malmaison Brasserie	2
Café Truva	12	Relish	9
Cruz	8	Restaurant Martin	
Daniel's	6	Wishart	11
Fishers	3	The Shore	5
King's Wark	10	The Vintner's Rooms	13
The Kitchin	7	Waterfront Wine Bar	4

ARGYLE ST.
HOPEFIELD TERR.
PRINCE REGENT ST.
N. JUNCTION ST.
CROMWELL ST.
COUPER ST.
CITADEL ST.
COBURG ST.
SANDPORT PL.
FERRY ROAD
MILL LANE
SHERIFF BRAE
COALHILL
THE SHORE
DOCK PL.
THE TOWER
TOWER ST.
TOWER ST. LANE
OCEAN DR
BUSH ST.
BERNARD ST.
CONSTITUTION STREET
BALTIC ST.
ASSEMBLY ST.
CADIZ ST.
SALAMANDER ST.
ELBE ST.
QUEEN CHARLOTTE STREET
GREAT JUNCTION STREET
KING ST.
CABLES WYND
YARDHEADS ST.
HENDERSON STREET
GILES ST.
CARFIELD
W. BOWLING GREEN ST.
BANGOR ROAD
BURLING ST.
JUNCTION PL.
PIRRIE ST.
KIRKGATE
JOHN'S LA.
JOHN'S PLACE
LINKS PLACE
POPLAR LANE
SALAMANDER ST.
ANDERSON PLACE
BONNINGTON ROAD
TENNANT ST.
KIRK ST.
CASSELB ST.
JANE STREET
ACADEMY ST.
DUKE STREET
DUNCAN PLACE
HERMITAGE PLACE
INDUSTRIAL RD
BURNS ST.
ROSEVALE TERR.
PRIMROSE ST.
LOCHEND ROAD
EASTER RD
GORDON ST.
MANDER ST.
LEITH WALK

0   200 yds

SHOPS	
Kinloch Anderson	b
Flux	c
Ocean Terminal	a

© Crown copyright

other than informal practice sessions by locals, there's no golf played on the Links these days. Instead, the tree-lined area of municipal park offers a stretch of green space for a walk or a play around.

Trinity House

99 Kirkgate ☎0131/554 3289, ⓦwww.historic-scotland.gov.uk. £4.

While Leith has a fair number of interesting old buildings, many are tucked away or obscured by more recent developments, and few are given the prominence accorded

to architectural and historical treasures elsewhere in the city. Trinity House is the only one of the port's grand buildings open to the public, but even here access is limited – all visits must be pre-booked on the number above, but if you're interested in maritime history, it's well worth the effort. The house is home of the Incorporation of Masters and Mariners of Leith, and was used in the medieval era as a mariners' hospice, funded by a tax on ships coming into the port. The present Neoclassical villa dates from 1816 and has some impressive original interiors and plasterwork, as well as a significant collection of maritime memorabilia, paintings and ships' models.

The Shore

The best way to absorb Leith's history and seafaring connections is to take a stroll along the Shore, a tenement-lined road running alongside the final stretch of the Water of Leith, just before it disgorges into the working docks area and, beyond that, the Firth of Forth. Until the mid-nineteenth century this was a bustling and cosmopolitan harbour, visited by ships from all over the world, but as vessels docking here became increasingly large, they moored up instead at custom-built docks built beyond the original quays; these days, the Shore has only a handful of boats permanently moored alongside. Instead, the focus of the Shore is on the numerous pubs and restaurants which line the street, many of which spill tables and chairs out onto the cobbled pavement on sunny days. A drink or snack at one of these places (see pp.133–135) is a great way to absorb the scene, but if you're taking a gentle amble along the length of the Shore it's well worth checking out some of the historic buildings, too, which include the imposing Neoclassical Custom House; the round signal tower above *Fishers* restaurant, which was originally constructed as a windmill; and the turrets and towers of the Sailors' Home, built in

Scots Baronial style in the 1880s as a dosshouse for seafarers, and now home to the rather swankier digs of the *Malmaison Hotel* (see p.165). If you walk on from here past the heavy steel girders of the 130-year-old Victoria Swing Bridge you'll get a good view of today's working docks, a mix of old warehouses, container loading bays and the seemingly unstoppable march of new housing.

Royal Yacht Britannia

Ocean Drive ☎0131/555 5566, ⓦwww.royalyachtbritannia.co.uk. Daily: April–Oct 9.30am–4.30pm; Nov–March 10am–3.30pm. £9.50.

Moored alongside Terence Conran's huge Ocean Terminal shopping and entertainment centre, *Britannia* is one of the world's most famous ships. Launched in 1953, she was used by the royal family for over 44 years for state visits, diplomatic functions, honeymoons and holidays; Leith's port operators acquired

▼ INSIDE THE ROYAL YACHT BRITANNIA

PLACES Leith

▲ NEWHAVEN LIGHTHOUSE

insights into life aboard even if you're not into loyal veneration: a full Marine Band was always part of the 300-strong crew; hand signals were used by the sailors to communicate orders as shouting was forbidden; and a special solid mahogany rail was built onto the royal bridge to allow the Queen to stand on deck as *Britannia* came into port, without fear of a gust of wind lifting the royal skirt.

her following decommission in 1997 against the wishes of many of the royals, who felt that scuttling would have been a more dignified end. Visits to *Britannia* begin in the visitor centre within Ocean Terminal, where royal holiday snaps and video clips of *Britannia* in various exotic foreign ports are shown. After this you're allowed on board, with the chance to wander around the bridge, admiral's quarters, officers' mess and state apartments. The ship has been largely kept as she was when in service, with a well-preserved 1950s dowdiness which the audioguide loyally attributes to the Queen's good taste and astute frugality in the lean postwar years. Certainly the atmosphere is a far cry from the opulent splendour which many expect.

While *Britannia* will inevitably captivate ardent royalists, the tour offers some entertaining

Newhaven

To the west of Leith lies the old village (now suburb) of Newhaven, established by James IV at the start of the sixteenth century as an alternative shipbuilding centre to Leith: his massive warship, the *Great Michael*, capable of carrying 120 gunners, 300 mariners and 1000 troops, and said to have used up all the trees in Fife, was built here. Newhaven has also been a ferry station and an important fishing centre, landing some six million oysters a year at the height of its success in the 1860s. Today, the chief pleasure here is a stroll around the stone harbour, which still has a pleasantly salty feel with a handful of boats tied up alongside or resting gently on the tidal mud. You might want to make a brief stop at the small Newhaven Heritage Museum (daily noon–4.45pm; free), which has a fairly homespun series of exhibits about the district's history of fishing and seafaring.

Trips out to Inchcolm Island (see p.153) on the Firth of Forth on board a high-speed RIB run from the harbour (daily April–Oct, £20; ☎0131/331 4857, ⓦwww.seafari.co.uk).

Shops

Kinloch Anderson

Commercial St ☎0131/555 1390, ⓦwww.kinlochanderson.com. Closed Sun. One of Edinburgh's larger kilt outfitters, with a large showroom full of tartan and the associated trimmings. Fairly conservative, so don't go in hoping to get hold of the *Braveheart* look.

Flux

55 Bernard St ☎0131/554 4075. ⓦwww.get2flux.co.uk. Interesting local arts and crafts, including pottery and funky glass lampshades as well as more mainstream, gimmicky knick-knacks.

Ocean Terminal

Ocean Drive ☎0131/558 8888, ⓦwww.oceanterminal.com. Leith's big retail destination, though with Debenhams and BHS as the headline department stores, it's not the most exciting shopping spot in the city. However, the presence of Gap, Kurt Muller, Fat Face and the FairTrade store Earth Squared makes things a bit more interesting.

Cafés

Café Truva

77 The Shore ☎0131/554 5502. Surprisingly, café culture hasn't really made it to Leith, but this Turkish-owned place just back from the water serves up decent sandwiches and snacks, as well as coffee made both in the Italian and in the Turkish way.

Relish

6 Commercial St ☎0131/476 1920. Leith's best deli, with some excellent cheeses, hams and treats if you want to make up your own sandwiches. The window stools are a nice spot for a coffee or a treat.

Restaurants

Britannia Spice

150 Commercial St ☎0131/555 2255, ⓦwww.britanniaspice.co.uk. Closed Sun lunch. The decor has a nautical theme, the decent, mid-priced food is prepared by specialist chefs from different parts of the subcontinent, and the awards for this relatively new but ambitious Indian restaurant have been piling up.

Daniel's

88 Commercial St ☎0131/553 5933, ⓦwww.daniels-bistro.co.uk. Likeable, well-run bistro in an attractive setting on the ground floor of a converted warehouse. Food is heartily French, with many dishes from the Alsace; the *tarte flambée*, one of the house specialities, is a simple but delicious onion and bacon pizza.

Fishers

1 The Shore ☎0131/554 5666, ⓦwww.fishersbistros.co.uk. One of the first wave of seafood bistros which put Leith's dining scene on the map, the menu here has an appealing range of expensive and fancy fish dishes, but there are also impressive bar-style snacks such as fishcakes and chowder. Reservations recommended.

PLACES

Leith

The Kitchin

78 Commercial Quay ☎0131/555 1755, ⓦwww.thekitchin.com. Closed Sun & Mon. Opened in 2006 by aptly-named young Scottish chef Tom Kitchin, and holder of a Michelin star little more than six months later, the restaurant puts itself at the more relaxed end of the fine-dining bracket and offers some tantalising dishes including rolled pig's head with crispy ear salad, or duck cooked whole.

Malmaison Brasserie

1 Tower Place ☎0131/468 5001, ⓦwww.malmaison.com. A successful attempt to re-create the feel of a stylish, mid-priced Parisian restaurant, serving excellent steak and chips as well as indulgent breakfasts and brunches.

Restaurant Martin Wishart

54 The Shore ☎0131/553 3557, ⓦwww.martin-wishart.co.uk. Closed Sun & Mon. The eponymous chef is one of the leading lights of the Scottish culinary scene, and was the first Michelin star holder in Edinburgh. Though relatively modest in size and demure in atmosphere, this place wows the gourmets with highly accomplished and exquisitely presented, French-influenced dishes featuring Scottish sourced fish and meat. A two-course lunch is £22.50, a seven-course evening tasting menu £60. Reservations recommended.

The Vintner's Rooms

87 Giles St ☎0131/554 6767, ⓦwww.thevintnersrooms.com. Closed Sun & Mon. Splendid restaurant in a seventeenth-century warehouse; the small but ornate Rococo dining room is a marvel, and the food isn't bad either; expect to pay £17–25 for mains such as pancetta-wrapped confit of monkfish with puy lentils or stuffed saddle of lamb.

Waterfront Wine Bar

1c Dock Place ☎0131/554 7427, ⓦwww.waterfrontwinebar.co.uk. Tasty seafood dishes, mostly mid-priced and not too fussy, served in a former lock-keeper's cottage which has been extended over the water to create a New England-style effect. You can eat in the wonderfully characterful wine bar or roomier conservatory at the back.

Pubs and bars

Cruz

14 The Shore ☎0131/553 6699, ⓦwww.thecruz.co.uk. Daily noon–1am. Situated right on the Water of Leith in a ship that has served as a minesweeper, luxury yacht,

▼ THE VINTNER'S ROOMS

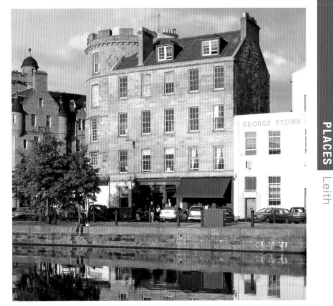

▲ LEITH WATERFRONT

and night club in previous incarnations, this floating style-bar is sleek and elegant inside and includes a sun terrace for classy al fresco cocktails during the summer months.

Kings Wark

36 The Shore ☎0131/554 9260. Sun–Thurs noon–11pm, Fri & Sat noon–midnight. Real ale in an atmospheric, restored eighteenth-century pub in prime position on the Shore, with impressive bar meals chalked up on the rafters.

The Shore

3–4 The Shore ☎0131/553 5080. Mon–Sat 11am–midnight, Sun 12.30–11pm. Traditional, well lived-in bar with an adjacent restaurant. There's regular live jazz or folk music as well as real ales and good bar snacks.

North and west Edinburgh

The sights and attractions to the north and west of Edinburgh's compact centre are more widely spread out, but the open spaces here provide a welcome break from the sometimes overwhelming history and architecture of the centre, and there's also the chance to discover the capital's seafront. The principal landmark on this side of the city is wooded Corstorphine Hill, whose lower slopes harbour Edinburgh Zoo, one of the city's most popular family attractions. Nearby there's Murrayfield Stadium, the largest sporting arena in the city, and Edinburgh's revitalized canal. Another of the villages now absorbed into Edinburgh's suburban sprawl, Cramond lies at the mouth of the River Almond and makes a great base for a bracing shoreline walk.

Edinburgh Zoo

Corstorphine Rd, Corstorphine
℗0131/334 9171, ⓦwww
.edinburghzoo.org.uk. Daily: April–Sept
9am–6pm; Oct & March 9am–5pm;
Nov–Feb 9am–4.30pm. £10.50. Buses
#12, #26 & #31 from Princes St, or
#100 from Waverley Bridge.

Established in 1913, Edinburgh's zoo has a long-established reputation for preserving rare and endangered species. The eighty-acre site is permanently packed with kids, and many of the facilities are imaginatively designed with education as well as play in mind – the climbing frame's position near the chimps enclosure allows parents to keep half an eye on both, and reflect on Edinburgh student Charles Darwin's theories of evolution. The general emphasis of the zoo is fast moving away from bored animals in cages to imaginatively designed habitats and viewing areas – the latter are best seen by taking a hilltop safari, a regular shuttle trip to the top of Corstorphine Hill in a Landrover-pulled trailer, which passes large enclosures full of camels and llamas. Once

▼ PENGUIN PARADE AT EDINBURGH ZOO

NORTH & WEST EDINBURGH

N

Firth of Forth

Cramond Island

Granton Harbour

Drum Sands

Tidal Causeway

1 Roman fort

WEST SHORE ROAD

SILVERKNOWES

LWR GRANTON RD A901

CRAMOND

Lauriston Castle

MUIRHOUSE PKWY

GRANTON ROAD

River Almond

CRAMOND RD SOUTH

SILVERKNOWES RD

FERRY ROAD

CRAMOND RD NTH

B9085

FERRY ROAD

BARNTON RDBT

QUEENSFERRY ROAD A90

HILLHOUSE ROAD

A902 TELFORD ROAD

Royal Botanic Garden

DRUM BRAE NORTH

DRUM BRAE SOUTH

CLERMISTON RD

A90

QUEENSFERRY ROAD

Western General Hospital

Corstorphine Hill

GLASGOW ROAD

A8 ST JOHN'S ROAD

CORSTORPHINE ROAD

A8

Water of Leith

2 St Mary's **8** WEST END

Edinburgh Zoo

BALGREEN ROAD

3 Haymarket Station

5 **6**

Edinburgh Quay **7**

SHOP
Helen Bateman Shoes **a**

Murrayfield

WEST APPROACH ROAD

DALRY RD

DUNDEE ST

MORRISON ST

GROSVENOR ST

HAYMARKET TCE

Hearts FC (Tynecastle Park)

UGC Fountain Park **8**

DALRY RD

EATING & DRINKING

Athletic Arms (The Diggers)	8	First Coast	6
Caley Sample Room	9	Restaurant at the Bonham	2
Cramond Inn	1	Sushiya	4
Dolce e Salato	5	The Skerries	
Embark	7	Seafood Restaurant	3

GORGIE ROAD

HUTCHISON RD

SLATEFORD ROAD

NEW MART RD

Caledonian Brewery

Napier University

Dominion Cinema

MORNINGSIDE RD

BRUNTSFIELD PL

Corn Exchange

Union Canal

COLINTON ROAD

0   400 yds

© Crown copyright

EICA:Ratho ◁

SHOP
Helen Bateman Shoes a

◁ South Queensferry & Old Cramond Bridge

Newhaven & Leith ▷

at the top, you can admire the city views, then wander back down past the African Plains Experience – an elevated wooden walkway out past some zebra and antelope grazing in fields which are, admittedly, rather more Midlothian than Maasai Mara – and a row of glass-walled pens containing various species of big cat. The zoo's most famous inhabitants are its penguins, a legacy of Leith's whaling trade in the South Atlantic. The penguin parade, which takes place daily at 2.15pm from April to September, and on sunny March and October days, has gained something of a cult status, with rangers encouraging a bunch of the flightless birds to leave their pen and waddle around a short circuit of pathways thronged with admiring and amused spectators.

Union Canal

ⓦ www.scottishcanals.co.uk. Buses #1 & #34 from Princes St stop at Edinburgh Quay. The Union Canal was built in 1822 to connect Edinburgh to Falkirk, where it joins the Forth & Clyde Canal which links Scotland's east and west coasts. As Scotland's canals in general fell into disuse during the twentieth century the Union Canal became scruffy, overgrown and generally ignored. A lot of money has been spent tidying up the canal in recent years, however, making it navigable once again to boats, and these days it is used by rowers, paddlers and even a few holiday makers on narrow boats. There's a handful of bars and restaurants at the newly built Edinburgh Quay at the canal terminus – one of many emerging developments in this area, and both walking and cycling are encouraged along the well-surfaced towpath. There aren't really any significant sights to look out for, though you'll normally encounter plenty of activity from the canal's resident ducks,

coots and swans. A couple of boats do operate trips on the canal, including Re-union (☎0845/345 7448, ⓦwww .re-union.org.uk) and the restaurant narrowboat *Zazou* (☎0131/669 5516, ⓦwww .zazoucruises.co.uk), but usually only for groups.

Murrayfield Stadium

Roseburn St, Murrayfield ☎0131/346 5000, ⓦwww.scottishrugby.org. Buses #12, #26, #31 from Princes St. Well-known to rugby union fans around the world, Murrayfield is where Scotland's home international fixtures are played. An impressive all-seat stadium holding 68,000 people, it's an exciting place to be when packed to the gills with singing, chanting fans on match-days, and has a different, if equally inspiring feel when empty; guided tours (book 48hr in advance; £5) offer a chance to poke around a few of the forbidden quarters of the arena, with a look at the commentary boxes, hospitality areas, dressing rooms and tunnel, concluding with a chance to take a player's-eye-view by walking (or running) out through the tunnel. A shop in the stadium concourse (Mon–Sat 9am–5pm) sells replica shirts, sports gear and souvenirs.

Lauriston Castle

Cramond Rd South, Davidson's Mains ☎0131/336 2060, ⓦwww .cac.org.uk. Admission by tour only: April–Oct Sat–Thurs 11am, noon, 2pm, 3pm, 4pm; Nov–March

▼ GATEPOST IN THE GROUNDS OF LAURISTON CASTLE

Sat & Sun noon, 2pm, 3pm. £5. Bus #24 from Princes or Frederick streets.

A country villa set in its own parkland on the fringes of Edinburgh's northwest urban sprawl, Lauriston Castle is a well-preserved, if fairly unglamorous, oddity. On first sight a neo-Jacobean riot of pointy turrets, crow-stepped gables and tall, thin chimneys, the "castle" is in fact a late sixteenth-century tower-house with extensive domestic additions from the 1820s and 1870s. At the turn of the twentieth century it was bought by a well-to-do Edinburgh couple, Mr and Mrs Reid, who upgraded and furnished it with all the mod cons of the early Edwardian era, including hot and cold running water, central heating and double glazing. They also filled the building with objects they liked or found technically accomplished, including some fine Italian furniture, Blue John glassware and seventeenth-century Dutch tapestries. On the death of Mrs Reid, the house and contents were gifted to Edinburgh Council, and have been preserved as a time capsule of that era. The mature grounds include an ornamental Japanese friendship garden and a series of croquet lawns from where there are pleasantly sylvan views out over the Firth of Forth.

▲ SWANS AT CRAMOND

Cramond

Buses #24 and #41 from George St.
Clustered on the eastern bank of the River Almond where it meets the Forth estuary, Cramond is one of the city's most atmospheric – and poshest – old villages. Popular with locals for Sunday afternoon seaside strolls, it's a great place to take in some sea air and explore the compact but charming series of step-gabled whitewashed houses which rise up from the riverside, interlaced with steep alleys and stairways. The best of the local walks are along the wide promenade which follows the shoreline, from where you get some great views of the Forth; or out across the causeway to the uninhabited bird sanctuary of Cramond Island – though be aware that the causeway disappears as high tide approaches and can leave

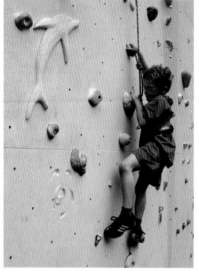

▲ CLIMBER AT EICA:RATHO

climbing wall. Having cost £24 million, the centre struggled financially until its recent rescue by Edinburgh Council. The spectacular vision of its architect founders was to enclose (and roof) a disused quarry, creating a giant arena that's now used for international climbing competitions as well as classes (from £20 for an hour-long taster session) for climbers of all levels, including beginners and kids. Above the arena, just under the glass roof, "Aerial Assault" (£8) is a stomach-churning, suspended obstacle course 100 metre off the ground, which you take on secured into a sliding harness. Elsewhere in this multi-faceted facility are a state-of-the-art gym and fitness studio, spa, Scrambles the climbing-themed kid's soft play area and a café which peers out over the climbing arena, as well as conferencing and events facilities too.

At the time of going to press no public transport linked to the centre; if you're driving, follow the signs from the Newbridge roundabout on the A8, not far from the airport.

you stranded if you get your timings wrong. For tide times, either check the noticeboard on shore (although this is sometimes vandalized) or call the Coastguard (☎01333/450 666). Inland of Cramond, there's another pleasant walk along a tree-lined path leading upstream along the River Almond, past former mills and their adjoining cottages towards the sixteenth-century Old Cramond Bridge.

EICA:Ratho

South Platt Hill, Ratho ☎0131/333 6333, ⊛www.eica-ratho.com. Mon–Fri 6.15am–10pm, Sat & Sun 10am–7pm, though hours differ for different facilities. Free entry; charges for activities vary.

Undoubtedly one of the modern wonders of Scottish sport, EICA:Ratho, or Edinburgh International Climbing Arena, is the world's largest indoor climbing facility, incorporating a remarkable 2400 square metres of artificial

Shops

Helen Bateman Shoes

16 William St, West End ☎0131/220 4495, ⊛www.helenbateman.com. Closed Sun. A chic boutique selling an exquisite range of

designer and bespoke ladies shoes. As sexy in the city as it gets in Edinburgh.

Cafés

Dolce e Salato

102 Dalry Rd ☎0131/346 0007.
Stunning Neapolitan *pasticceria* serving all kinds of Italian cakes, sweets, pastries and pizzas. Just a few seats inside, but great for take-away picnics and you can peer through a window into the bakery behind.

Restaurants

Embark

Edinburgh Quay ☎0131/222 4898, ⓦwww.embarkonline.co.uk. Best of the venues to locate at the new Edinburgh Quay development overlooking the terminus of the Union Canal. Decent modern bistro-style food is served in the fresh-looking bar downstairs or bright first-floor restaurant.

First Coast

101 Dalry Rd ☎0131/313 4404, ⓦwww.first-coast .co.uk. Closed Sun.
Mellow, moderately priced bistro well-run by a young staff and serving tasty dishes based around good Scottish produce such as Aberdeen Angus beef or sustainable fish.

Restaurant at the Bonham

35 Drumsheugh Gardens ☎0131/623 9319, ⓦwww .thebonham.com. Elegant but modern dining space in one of Edinburgh's most attractive contemporary hotels, with good local sourcing in evidence from imaginative French chef Michel Bouyer. Moderate to expensive.

The Skerries Seafood Restaurant

Dunstane House Hotel, 4 West Coates, Haymarket ☎0131/337 5320, ⓦwww .dunstane-hotel-edinburgh.co.uk.
Meat and (memorably) seafood direct from the verdant shores of the Orkney Isles, available both in the bar and in the smarter, more expensive hotel restaurant.

Sushiya

19 Dalry Rd ☎0131/313 3222, ⓦwww.sushiya.co.uk. Closed Tues.
The best sushi and Japanese

PLACES North and west Edinburgh

▼ THE CALEDONIAN BREWERY

food in Edinburgh at the moment, set in a slightly edgy, Tokyo-style bar complete with high tables and chaotic Japanese TV shows.

Pubs and bars

Athletic Arms (The Diggers)

1–3 Angle Park Terrace, Gorgie ☎0131/337 3822. Mon–Thurs noon–midnight, Fri & Sat noon–1am, Sun 12.30–6pm. Known to all as *The Diggers* after the spade-wielding employees of the cemetery across the road, this is a place of pilgrimage if you're into sport (Murrayfield and Hearts' Tynecastle ground are just along the road) and real ale, with the Caledonian Brewery's beers well represented.

Caley Sample Room

58 Angle Park Terrace, Gorgie ☎0131/337 7204, ⓦwww .thecaleysampleroom.co.uk. Mon–Thurs 11am–midnight, Fri & Sat 11am–1am, Sun 11am–11pm. Although there's no official link, this is a good spot to taste the cask ales of the nearby Caledonian Brewery, and there's some decent food available too.

Cramond Inn

30 Cramond Glebe Rd, Cramond ☎0131/336 2035. Mon–Thurs 11am–11pm, Fri & Sat 11am–midnight, Sun 12.30–11pm. This old inn by the riverside at Cramond is the perfect place for a drink or a pub meal after a stroll along the coastal path.

South Edinburgh

South Edinburgh begins at the open spaces of the Meadows, just beyond the university, from where suburbs stretch out to old Midlothian mining towns and the significant elevation of the Pentland Hills. The leafy, mainly Victorian suburbs closest to town hold many student digs and guesthouses, although there's no doubt that the refined essence of Miss Jean Brodie, who was in her prime in this part of town, lingers on. Beyond these, the green patches of the south's numerous hills offer some pleasant walking routes, though you'll need to catch a bus to get out to the most interesting of the sights, the Rosslyn Chapel, Scotland's most mysterious medieval church.

The Meadows

Like the Old Town's Princes Street Gardens (see p.100), the area of parkland known as the Meadows was once a shallow loch. Drained in the eighteenth century, its sheltered swathes of grass are well utilized for games of tennis, cricket and football, though they're just as popular as a pleasant through-route to or from the Southside, with lovely blossoms appearing on the trees in spring and grand views up to Arthur's Seat. On the southwest corner of the Meadows is the slightly more elevated land of Bruntsfield Links, another of Edinburgh's early golf courses, which now operates as a 36-hole pitch-and-putt course in the summer (April–Sept; free; clubs and balls can be hired from the Golf Tavern; see p.148).

Craigmillar Castle

Craigmillar Castle Rd, Craigmillar ☎0131/661 4445, Ⓦwww .historic-scotland.gov.uk. April–Sept daily 9.30am–5.30pm; Oct–March Sat–Wed 9.30am–4.30pm. £4. Bus #8, #33 or #49 from North Bridge to Edinburgh Royal Infirmary, then a ten-minute walk along a footpath to the castle.

Set in a green belt around five miles southeast of Edinburgh's centre, Craigmillar is a classic medieval ruined fortress. Before Queen Victoria set her heart on Balmoral, Craigmillar was considered for the role of her royal castle north of the border, a possibility which seems somewhat odd now given its proximity to an ugly council housing scheme, also called Craigmillar, one of Edinburgh's most deprived districts. That

▼ STROLLING THROUGH THE MEADOWS

© Crown copyright

Pentland Hills, Hillend ▽ & Flotterstone   Rosslyn Chapel ▽ & Penicuik   Mining Museum ▽ & Dalkeith

SOUTH EDINBURGH

SHOP
Falko Konditormeister **a**

EATING & DRINKING		
The Apartment	**1**	Golf Tavern	**2**
Borough Hotel	**5**	The New Bell	**6**
The Canny Man's	**9**	S. Luca	**8**
Celadon	**4**	Sweet Melinda's	**3**
		Toast	**7**

said, the immediate setting feels very rural and Craigmillar enjoys splendid views back to Arthur's Seat and Edinburgh Castle. The oldest part of the complex is the L-shaped tower house, which dates back to the early 1400s – this remains substantially intact, and the great hall, with its resplendent late Gothic chimneypiece, is in good enough shape to be rented out for functions. The tower house was surrounded in the 1500s by a quadrangular wall with cylindrical corner towers and was used on occasion by Mary, Queen of Scots. It was abandoned to its picturesque decay in the mid-eighteenth century, and today the peaceful ruins and their adjoining grassy lawns make for a great place to explore, with kids in particular loving the run of their very own castle.

Royal Observatory

Blackford Hill, ☏0131/668 8404, ⓦwww.roe.ac.uk. Bus #41 from George IV Bridge. Incorporating a house for the Astronomer Royal for Scotland as well as a beautiful library and a university department, the Royal Observatory remains an important international centre for research, some of which involves the remote operation of telescopes in Australia and Hawaii. It isn't generally open to the public other than for the occasional talk or open day as well as its Friday evening stargazing sessions (usually 7–8.45pm; £4), when you can make use of the solar and astronomical telescopes and learn a bit more about the night sky. Nonetheless, the building makes an impressive contribution to the profile of Blackford Hill, another of the prime viewpoints on the south side of Edinburgh. The long, dark evenings of winter are the best time to join one of the public sessions, though in summer there's a chance to hunt for sun spots or the Northern Lights.

Hermitage of Braid

Hermitage Drive, Braid Hills ⓦ www .edinburgh.gov.uk/cecrangerservice. Visitor centre Mon–Thurs 9am–5pm, Fri 9am–4pm, Sun noon–5pm. Free. Bus #11, #15 or #16 from Lothian Rd. At the foot of Blackford Hill, the bird sanctuary of Blackford Pond is the starting point for one of the many trails running through the Hermitage of Braid nature reserve, a lovely shady area along the course of the Braid Burn, after which it is named, which offers some quiet waterside walks. The castellated eighteenth-century mansion on the burn's bank now serves as a visitor centre; it's mostly aimed at school

▲ HIGHLAND COW IN THE GROUNDS OF THE PRESTONFIELD HOTEL

groups, but you can get some background information on the trails, trees, plants and local wildlife. Immediately to the south are the Braid Hills, most of which are occupied by two golf courses, closed on alternate Sundays in order to allow access for walkers.

The Pentland Hills

ⓦ www.edinburgh.gov.uk/phrp. Hillend: buses #4 and #15 from Princes St; Flotterstone: McEwans coach #100 from Princes St. Dominating most views of south Edinburgh, the Pentland Hills

PLACES South Edinburgh

▼ HIKERS IN THE PENTLAND HILLS

PLACES

South Edinburgh

▲ ROSSLYN CHAPEL

are an elevated chain, some eighteen miles long and five miles wide, which offer walkers and mountain bikers a thrilling taste of wild Scottish countryside just a few miles beyond the city suburbs. Numerous bike trails and walks, from gentle strolls along well-marked paths to a ten-mile traverse of the hills and moors, are outlined in a free pamphlet available from the Regional Park Information Centre at Flotterstone, a former staging post ten miles south of the city centre on the A702. The simplest way to get a taste of the scenery of the Pentlands is to set off from the car park by the ski centre at Hillend at the northeast end of the range; take the path up the right-hand side of the dry ski slopes, turning left shortly after crossing a stile to reach a prominent point with outstanding views over Edinburgh and Fife. If you're feeling energetic, the views get even better higher up, and you'll get more of an idea of the unexpected green emptiness of the Pentland range running away to the south.

Rosslyn Chapel

Roslin ☎ 0131/440 2159, ⓦ www
.rosslynchapel.org.uk. Mon–Sat
9am–6pm, Sun noon–4.45pm, closes
5pm in winter months. £7. Bus #15
from St Andrew Square.

Seven miles south of Edinburgh's centre, tranquil Roslin village has two unusual claims to fame: the world's first cloned sheep, Dolly, was created here at the Roslin Institute in 1997, and the mysterious, richly decorated late-Gothic Rosslyn Chapel. The latter was intended to be a huge collegiate church dedicated to St Matthew, but construction halted soon after the founder's death in 1484, and the vestry built onto the facade nearly four hundred years later is the sole subsequent addition. After a long period of neglect, a massive restoration project has recently been undertaken, with a rigid canopy constructed over the chapel in order to dry out the saturated ceiling and walls. Visitors are free to look around both inside and out: Rosslyn's exterior bristles with pinnacles, gargoyles, flying buttresses and canopies, while inside the stonework is, if anything, even more intricate. The foliage carving is particularly outstanding, with botanically accurate depictions of over a dozen different leaves and plants. Among them are cacti and Indian corn, compounding the legend that the founder's grandfather, the daring sea adventurer Prince Henry of Orkney, did indeed set foot in the New World a century before Columbus. The greatest and most original carving of all is the extraordinary knotted Apprentice Pillar; it's said to have been made by an apprentice during the absence of the master mason, who killed him in a fit of jealousy on seeing the finished work. The imagery of the carvings around the chapel, together with the history of the family which owns it, the St Clairs of Rosslyn, leave little doubt about its links to the Knights Templar and freemasonry; the chapel is also regularly drawn into conspiracy theories on these themes, most prominently recently in Dan Brown's best-seller *The Da Vinci Code*; the chapel's appearance in the film of the same name precipitated a huge surge in visitor numbers which detracts a little from the mysterious air of the place.

Scottish Mining Museum

Lady Victoria Colliery, Newtongrange ☎0131/663 7519, ⓦwww .scottishminingmuseum.org. Daily: Feb–Oct 10am–5pm; Nov–Jan 10am–4pm. £5.95. Lothian Buses #3A and #29 from Princes St or North Bridge, or First Edinburgh #X81 from Princes St and #X95 from St Andrew Square.

This industrial heritage museum dedicated to the many collieries found in this area of Scotland is a particularly enjoyable place for kids, its mine and the local community brought to life via "magic helmets" – essentially remote control headphones – which allow you to follow the progress of a shift arriving at the mine and get a taste of the slightly surreal life below ground. Ex-miners now work as tour guides, explaining the origins of coal, what went on at the pithead above the 1625-Metre shaft, and the Victorian winding tower, still in working order, which is powered by Scotland's largest steam engine.

Shops

Falko Konditormeister

7 Bruntsfield Rd ☎0131/656 0763. Tues–Fri noon–7pm, Sat 9am–5pm. A brilliant German baker (a Konditormeister is a qualified master confectioner) who produces memorable cakes, tarts, pretzels and bread.

Cafés

Toast

146 Marchmont Rd, Marchmont ☎0131/446 9873. Closed Mon evening. Café culture hits the student fiefdom of deepest Marchmont, in a relaxed and stylish venue serving coffees and impressive lunchtime and evening light meals such as toasted focaccia and creamy chicken laksa.

S. Luca

16 Morningside Rd, Morningside ☎0131/446 0233, ⓦwww.s-luca .co.uk. Family-oriented city outlet for this much loved ice-cream maker from Musselburgh, whose 100-year old recipe doesn't use much more than double cream, milk and butter, and is made freshly every day. You could also try Irn Bru-flavoured sorbet (or the original drink, of course), knickerbocker glories, simple pasta dishes and panini, all served until 9.30pm every night.

Restaurants

The Apartment

7–13 Barclay Place (Bruntsfield Place), Bruntsfield ☎0131/228 6456. Hugely popular, highly fashionable modern diner, with chic furniture, sleek waiting staff and abstract modern art on the walls. Their "Chunky, Healthy

▲ SWEET MELINDA'S

A neat, straightforward seafood restaurant in a single, timber-panelled room with a friendly neighbourhood feel. It's edging towards the expensive side, but it's worth shelling out for dishes such as mackerel served with chorizo, or beautifully fried squid.

Pubs and bars

Borough Hotel
72–80 Causewayside ☎0131/668 2255. Mon–Thurs 11am–midnight, Fri & Sat 11–1am, Sun noon–1am. Contemporary boutique hotel with a large, easy-going bar and attached restaurant. A good choice of bar food that's well above average, with Sunday brunches in particular worth stopping in for.

The Canny Man's
239 Morningside Rd, Morningside ☎0131/447 1484. Mon–Wed 11.30am–11pm, Thurs–Sat 11.30am–midnight, Sun 12.30–11pm. Idiosyncratic pub-cum-museum adorned with anything that can be hung on the walls or from the ceiling. Local ales and over 200 whiskies on offer, as well as snacks. A brass plaque outside stating "No smoking, no credit cards, no mobile phones, no cameras, no backpackers" sets the tone.

Golf Tavern
30–31 Wrights Houses, Bruntsfield Links. Daily 10am–1am. A recently made-over bar with a golf theme, set in what's actually quite a historic local tavern. If photos of golfer Ernie Els alongside cool chocolate-brown sofas sounds a bit incongruous, they are, but you can sit outside and watch the pitch-and-putt golf, with Arthur's Seat as the backdrop.

Lines" feature filling kebabs of meat, fish or vegetables.

Celadon
49–51 Causewayside ☎0131/667 1110. Closed Sun lunch. Thai dining that's on its way upmarket, with well-judged dishes such as *prig prow* seafood and a surprisingly refined and tasteful setting with exposed stone walls and attractive artwork.

The New Bell
233 Causewayside, Newington ☎0131/668 2868, ⓦwww.thenewbell .com. A cosy, pleasant restaurant located above a pub, serving tasty meat and fish dishes that are streets ahead of standard pub fare. Mains such as baked cod or roast guinea fowl cost £15–18, and they're followed by crowd-pleasing desserts such as banana tarte tatin.

Sweet Melinda's
11 Roseneath St, Marchmont ☎0131/229 7953, ⓦwww .sweetmelindas.co.uk. Closed Sun all day & Mon lunch.

South Queensferry and the Forth Bridges

The famous Forth Rail Bridge is commonly regarded as an icon of Edinburgh, despite the fact that it's actually located eight miles northwest of the city centre over the narrowest point of the Firth of Forth, the estuary of the Forth river which rises in central Scotland and flows out to the North Sea. At the southern end of the bridge is the historic town of South Queensferry which, despite the drone of traffic passing over the road bridge, is an extremely pleasant spot on the water's edge. It serves as the focal point for visiting the local attractions, which include two grand stately houses and a wonderful ruined abbey on Inchcolm Island.

South Queensferry

Named for the saintly wife of King Malcolm Canmore, Margaret, whose chapel sits at the highest point of Edinburgh Castle, South Queensferry is a great place for a wander, with the firth on one side and a palpably historic air. The narrow, cobbled High Street is lined with tightly packed, brightly painted old buildings with pantile roofs, most of which date from the seventeenth and eighteenth centuries. The most dramatic is a black-harled, step-gabled house known as the Black Castle, built in 1626 for a sea captain; on either side of this the south side of the street has a two-tier arrangement, with arcaded shops below and a walkway for the upper houses running along the top of the shops. Only one row of houses separates the High Street from the water; through the gaps between these there's a great perspective of the two Forth bridges, an old stone harbour and a curved, pebbly

Getting to South Queensferry

It's relatively easy to get to South Queensferry by public transport. Bus #43 operated by First Edinburgh runs frequently from Princes Street to South Queensferry, while all trains to Dunfermline, Kirkcaldy and Dundee from central Edinburgh stop at Dalmeny station, from where there's a long flight of steps down to Hawes Pier or a well-signposted half-mile walk to the centre of town. In addition, Lothian Buses offer a Forth Bridges Cruise incorporating a bus tour from Waverley Bridge to South Queensferry and a boat cruise out to Inchcolm (☎0870/118 1866, ⓦwww.forthtours.com; £15) on the *Forth Belle*, with an option to go ashore on the island (£4.50).

North Queensferry & Fife

Inchcolm Island

Firth of Forth

N

Forth Road Bridge

Forth Rail Bridge

Hawes Pier

Ticket office for Inchcolm Island

Queensferry Museum

Black Castle

SOCIETY RD HOPETOUN RD WALKER DRIVE

HOPETOUN ROAD

THE LOAN

HIGH STREET

STONEYCROFT RD

EDINBURGH ROAD

HAWES BRAE

BO'NESS ROAD

MORISON GARDENS

STEWART TERRACE

STATION ROAD

VIEWFORTH

KIRKLISTON ROAD

BURGESS ROAD

LAWSON CRES

ROSEBERY AVENUE

DUNDAS AVENUE

STEWART CLARK AV

LOVERS' LANE

Dalmeny Station

ECHLINE TER KNOX CROOK STONEYFLATS CRESCENT INCHCOLM TER

ECHLINE AVENUE

ECHLINE AVE

BUILYEON ROAD

FERRYMUIR ROAD

A90

MOUBRAY GR

SCOTSTOUN AVENUE

KIRKLISTON ROAD

Hopetoun House &

Dalmeny Estate

Dalmeny Village, Dalmeny House & Cramond Brig

SOUTH QUEENSFERRY & FORTH BRIDGES

0   200 yds

EATING & DRINKING

The Boathouse	2
Ferry Tap	5
The Grill at Dakota Forthbridge	6
Hawes Inn	3
Orocco Pier	1
Stables Tearoom	4

Edinburgh

© Crown copyright

beach, the scene each New Year's Day of the teeth-chattering "Loony Dook" (see p.180), when a gaggle of hung-over locals (along with some foolhardy tourists) charge into the sea for the quickest of dips.

Queensferry Museum

High St, South Queensferry
℡ 0131/331 5545, ⓦ www.cac.org
.uk. Mon & Thurs–Sat 10am–1pm
& 2.15–5pm, Sun noon–5pm. Free.
In the rather mundane setting of four upper-floor rooms of council offices, this charming collection of local history and artefacts is worth seeking out just to find out more about the Burry Man, a bizarre ceremony which takes place in Queensferry every August in which a local man is covered from head to toe in burrs (the spiky seed cases of the burdock plant), then walked around the streets to ward off evil spirits. In a room on the seaward side of the building there's also a big bay window with binoculars and telescopes provided for those who want to give bridges, boats and birds a closer inspection, while nearby boards provide some background on how the mighty Forth bridges were built.

▼ SOUTH QUEENSFERRY

Dalmeny House

Dalmeny Estate, South Queensferry ☎0131/331 1888, ⊛www.dalmeny .co.uk. July & Aug Mon, Tues & Sun 2–5.30pm. £5.50. Set on a 2000-acre estate between Cramond and South Queensferry, Dalmeny House is not, in truth, the prettiest country seat you'll encounter in Scotland, its Tudor-Gothic style giving rather too much prominence to castellations, towers and chimney stacks. As it's the seat and residence of the Earl of Rosebery, entry is quite restrictive, with viewing via tours only (generally on the hour and half-hour), but the quality of the items on show combined with the intriguing history of the family make it a fascinating place to visit. The fifth earl (1847–1929), a nineteenth-century British Prime Minister, married the heiress Hannah de Rothschild, and their union is the principal reason why Dalmeny boasts some the finest baroque and Neoclassical furniture produced for Louis XIV, XV and XVI during the hundred years before the French Revolution. Also in the collection are a very rare set of tapestries made from cartoons by Goya, and portraits by Raeburn, Reynolds, Gainsborough and Lawrence as well as a valuable collection of memorabilia relating to Napoleon Bonaparte, who clearly fascinated the fifth Earl – the collection includes the desk Napoleon used on St Helena, and his ornate shaving stand.

Hopetoun House

South Queensferry ☎0131/331 2451, ⊛www.hopetounhouse.com. April–Sept daily 10.30am–5pm. £8.
Sitting in its own extensive estate on the south shore of

▲ HOPETOUN HOUSE

the Forth, just to the west of South Queensferry, Hopetoun House ranks as one of the most impressive stately homes in Scotland. The original house was built at the turn of the eighteenth century for the first Earl of Hopetoun by Sir William Bruce, the architect of Holyroodhouse. A couple of decades later, William Adam carried out an enormous extension, engulfing the structure with a curvaceous main facade and two projecting wings – superb examples of Roman Baroque pomp and swagger. The scale and lavishness of Adam's interiors, most of whose decoration was carried out by his sons after the architect's death, make for a stark contrast with the intimacy of those designed by Bruce – the Red and Yellow Drawing Rooms, with their splendid ceilings by the young Robert Adam, are particularly impressive. Hopetoun's architecture is undoubtedly its most compelling feature, but the furnishings aren't completely overwhelmed, with some impressive seventeenth-century tapestries, Meissen porcelain, and a distinguished collection of paintings, including portraits by Gainsborough, Ramsay and Raeburn. The house's grounds are equally splendid, with a long, regal driveway and lovely walks along woodland trails and the banks of the Forth, as well as plenty of places for a picnic.

The Forth Bridges

Dominating South Queensferry and this section of the Forth are the two mighty, if contrasting, bridges. The more compelling is the formidable Rail Bridge, built from 1883 to 1890, which ranks among the supreme achievements of Victorian engineering. Plans for a suspension bridge to carry the railway line were ripped up in 1879 when the collapse of the Tay Rail Bridge, with the loss of around 100 lives, demanded some serious rethinking. The revised plans by Sir John Fowler and Benjamin Baker created a cantilevered structure over twice as strong as it actually needed to be. Some 50,000 tons of steel were used in the construction of a design that manages to express grace as well as might: the great French engineer Alexandre-Gustave Eiffel described it as "the greatest wonder of the century", although the artist William Morris did opine that it was "the supreme specimen of all ugliness". Less than half a mile to the west is the parallel and rather more prosaic Road Bridge, whose suspension format was derived from American models such as the Golden Gate Bridge. Completed in 1964, the road bridge finally killed off the 900-year-old ferry, but it's ageing fast under heavy traffic volume and there's now serious talk of the need for a second bridge, or possibly a replacement tunnel. The only way to cross the rail bridge is aboard a train heading to or from Edinburgh, though inevitably this doesn't allow much of a perspective of the spectacle itself. For the best panorama, make use of the pedestrian and cycle lane on the east side of the road bridge. You can get some background on both bridges at the South Queensferry Museum (see p.150), which reveals such various mind-boggling statistics as the number of rivets in the

▼ FORTH RAIL BRIDGE

▲ MAID OF THE FORTH INFORMATION BOARD

rail bridge (six and a half million), and that a shower of rain adds around 100 tons to its weight.

Inchcolm Island

☎ 01383/823 332, ⓦ www.historic-scotland.gov.uk. Boats run by: *Maid of the Forth* (☎ 0131/331 4857, ⓦ www.maidoftheforth.co.uk; April–Oct 2–3 trips daily; £13.50 including landing fee) and *Forth Belle* (☎ 0870/118 1866, ⓦ www.forthtours.com; £19.50 including bus from Edinburgh and landing fee).

Some five miles northeast of South Queensferry and reachable via a half-hour boat trip which departs from Hawes Pier at South Queensferry, Inchcolm is the most intriguing and attractive island in the Firth of Forth. The primary draw is the chance to explore the island's abbey, the best-preserved medieval monastic complex in Scotland, although the hour-and-a-half you're given ashore by the boat timetables also allows time for a picnic on the abbey's lawns or the chance to explore Inchcolm's old military fortifications and its extensive bird-nesting grounds. The abbey was founded in 1235 after King Alexander I was stormbound on the island and took refuge in a hermit's cell, and an order of Augustinian monks lived here until the abbey's religious function was curtailed by the Reformation in 1560. The structure as a whole is half-ruined today, but the explorable cluster of buildings include an intact tower, octagonal chapterhouse and echoing cloisters; from different parts of the abbey, tiny windows offer unexpected glimpses of the sea with Edinburgh's distinctive skyline in the distance. Aside from the abbey, Inchcolm also offers some short walks along paths which crisscross the island, some of which take you past the old installations that are the sole legacy of Inchcolm's one-time incarnation as a military base – gun emplacements, lookout posts and storehouses from both world wars still stand. The paths also afford some attractive views of the Firth, as well as the chance to see some of the island's principal inhabitants, birds – terns, oystercatchers, snipe, kittiwake and raucous gull all nest here at various times in the year. Seals can often be seen basking on the tidal reefs offshore and if you're lucky, you'll see dolphins and porpoises from the boat crossing to the island. A high-speed RIB also runs a ferry service (£20) to the island from Newhaven harbour (see p.132) beside Leith.

Cafés

Stables Tearoom

Hopetoun House, South Queensferry ☎ 0131/331 3661. April–Sept daily 10.30am–5pm. Classy lunches and afternoon teas with waitress service beside the stately home, even if it is located in the place where the horses used to get their nosebags.

▲ THE BOATHOUSE

Restaurants

The Boathouse

19b High St, South Queensferry
℡0131/331 5429, ⓦwww
.the-boathouse.info.
So close to the water that at
high tide the waves lap the walls
of the restaurant, which also
incorporates a wine bar and deli.
The cosy dining room enjoys
great views out to the bridges;
the seafaring theme is continued
through the menu, which
is dominated by moderately
expensive but classy seafood,
much of it local.

The Grill at Dakota Forthbridge

Dakota Forthbridge Hotel, Ferrymuir
Retail Park, South Queensferry
℡0870/423 4293, ⓦwww
.dakotaforthbridge.co.uk. Decent
modern dining with lots of
interesting seafood in this
stylish hotel chain conceived
by Malmaison founder Ken
McCulloch.

Orocco Pier

17 High St, South Queensferry
℡0131/331 1298, ⓦwww.oroccopier
.co.uk. The presence of a style
bar in South Queensferry
may seem a bit incongruous,
but this new place has wowed
everyone with its great setting
looking out to the bridges,
slick contemporary style and
moderately priced bistro food,
which ranges from steaks to
Thai-style mussels.

Pubs and bars

Ferry Tap

36 High St, South Queensferry
℡0131/331 2000. Mon–Thurs
11am–11.30pm, Fri & Sat
11–12.30am, Sun 12.30–11.30pm.
The local's favourite, slap in
the middle of the historic high
street, serving well-tended real
ales and simple but satisfying bar
food every lunchtime but only
on Mon, Wed and Fri evenings.

Hawes Inn

Newhalls Rd, South Queensferry
℡0131/331 1990. Mon–Sat
11am–11pm, Sun 12.30–10.30pm. An
old wayfarers' inn most famously
visited by Robert Louis
Stevenson, who used it in his
adventure story *Kidnapped*. Now
run by a national chain, there's
a predictability to the fare and
interior style, but its location is
a classic spot at the head of a
stone jetty right underneath the
Rail Bridge.

Accommodation

Hotels, guesthouses and B&Bs

As befits its status as a busy tourist city and important commercial centre, Edinburgh has a greater choice of accommodation than any other place in Britain outside London. **Hotels** (and large backpacker hostels; see p.166) are essentially the only options you'll find right in the heart of the city, but within relatively easy reach the selection of **guesthouses**, **B&Bs** and **campus accommodation** broadens considerably. **Prices** here are significantly higher than elsewhere in Scotland, with double rooms starting at £60 per night. Budget hotel chains offer the best value if you want basic accommodation right in the centre, with rooms available for £60–80; £80–100 per night will get you something more interesting and stylish. Note that many guesthouses and small hotels are located in Georgian or Victorian townhouses, most of which have three or more floors and no lift and so are not ideal if stairs are a problem. Bear in mind also that advance **reservations** are worthwhile at any time and very strongly recommended for stays during the Festival and around Hogmanay. The Scottish tourist board operates a central booking centre for accommodation all over the country, including Edinburgh; call ☎0845 225 5121 or visit ⓦwww.visitscotland.com. There's a £3 fee for this service, waived if you book online.

The Royal Mile

Bank Hotel 1 South Bridge ☎0131/622 6800, ⓦwww.festival-inns.co.uk. Notable location in a 1920s bank at the crossroads of the Royal Mile and South Bridge, with *Logie Baird's* bar downstairs and nine unusual but comfortable rooms upstairs on the theme of famous Scots. Doubles from £80.

Gladstone's Land 477b Lawnmarket, c/o National Trust for Scotland, 5 Charlotte Square ☎0131/243 9331, ⓦwww .nts.org.uk. Two classic Old Town apartments on the fourth floor of the historic Gladstone's Land (see p.67). Set up for self-catering, both sleep two in twin beds, and there's a minimum stay of three nights. £435 per week.

Ibis Edinburgh Centre 6 Hunter Square ☎0131/240 7000, ⓦwww.accorhotels .com. Probably the best-located chain hotel cheapie in the Old Town, within sight of the Royal Mile; rooms are modern and inexpensive, but there are few facilities other than a small bar. Doubles from £99.

A guide to prices

For hotels, guesthouses and B&Bs, the prices quoted in this chapter are for the cheapest double room in the summer high season, and include breakfast unless otherwise specified. Prices often rise during the Festival and over New Year (Hogmanay). Cheaper rates can sometimes be found if you visit outside high season, book online, or at the last minute. For hostels, we've given the standard price of a dorm bed in high season, as well as the cost of a private (double or twin) room, where available; neither rate includes breakfast.

CENTRAL EDINBURGH (ACCOMMODATION)

Royal Botanic Garden

INVERLEITH TERRACE

WATER OF LEITH WALKWAY

GLENOGLE ROAD

EYRE PLACE

Academicals RUFC

Grange Cricket Ground

HENDERSON ROW

STOCKBRIDGE

RAEBURN PLACE

FETTES ROW

ROYAL

CUMBERLAND STREET

GREAT KING STREET

Theatre Workshop

NEW TOWN

DEAN STREET

ROYAL CIRCUS PLACE

NORTHUMBERLAND ST

DEAN TERRACE

CIRCUS

DEAN VILLAGE

QUEENSFERRY ROAD

Georgian House

QUEEN STREET

Assembly Rooms

West Register House

GEORGE STREET

Floral Clock

NTS Headquarters

PRINCES STREET

Ross Bandstand

WEST END

St John

West Princes Street Gardens

St Cuthbert

OLD TOWN

St Mary's

The Castle

Traverse Theatre

Usher Hall

Dance Base

Filmhouse

Royal Lyceum Theatre

Edinburgh Conference Centre

Odeon Cinema

HAYMARKET

TOLLCROSS

Haymarket Train Station

Cameo Cinema

King's Theatre

Bruntsfield Links

ACCOMMODATION (cont.)

Melvin House Hotel	24	Royal Mile	
Novotel Edinburgh		Backpackers	31
Centre	49	St Christopher's Inn	27
Old Waverley Hotel	19	Scotsman Hotel, The	26
Point Hotel	48	Sheraton Grand	44
Premier Travel Inn	47	Six Mary's Place	6
Ramsays Bed &		Smart City Hostel	39
Breakfast	5	Tailors Hall Hotel	42
Regent House Hotel	9	Ten Hill Place Hotel	45
Rick's Restaurant		Tigerlily	21
with Rooms	18	Travelodge Edinburgh	
Royal Garden		Central	37
Apartments	16	Witchery Apartments, The	41

© Crown copyright

The Scotsman Hotel 20 North Bridge ☏0131/556 5565, ⊛www .thescotsmanhotel.co.uk. This plush, smart but non-stuffy new occupant of the grand old offices of the Scotsman news paper is one of Edinburgh's headline hotels. It's five-star stuff with modern gadgets and fittings, but the marble stair-case and walnut-panelled lobby have been retained, and you can sleep in the editor's old office. Doubles from £270.

Travelodge Edinburgh Central 33 St Mary's St ☏0870/191 1637, ⊛www .travelodge.co.uk. There's more than a hint of concrete brutalism about the look of this chain hotel, but it's well priced, and well located, 100yds from the Royal Mile oppo-site a clutch of decent restaurants. Doubles from £70, breakfast not included.

The Witchery Apartments Castlehill ☏0131/225 5613, ⊛www.thewitchery .com. Seven riotously indulgent suites grouped around this famously spooky res-taurant just downhill from the castle; expect strange antiques, big leather armchairs, tapestry-draped beds, oak panelling and huge roll-top baths, as well as ultra-modern sound systems and complimentary bottles of champagne. Top of the range, unique and memorable. Suites from £295.

Holyrood and Arthur's Seat

Holyrood Aparthotel 1 Nether Bake-house Close, Holyrood ☏0131/524 3200, ⊛www.holyroodaparthotel.com. A block of two-bedroom self-catering apartments near the new Scottish Parliament. The loca-tion has lots of Old Town atmosphere, and the accommodation is slick and modern with most mod cons. Apartments from £138 (two people sharing).

University of Edinburgh Pollock Halls of Residence 18 Holyrood Park Rd, Newington ☏0131/651 2007, ⊛www .edinburghfirst.com. Unquestionably the best setting of any of the city's university accommodation, right beside the Royal Commonwealth Swimming Pool and Holy-rood Park, and with a range of accommoda-tion from single rooms (£29), twins (£69)

and en-suite doubles (£74) to self-catering flats (from £340 per week). Available Easter and June to mid-Sept only.

South of the Royal Mile

Apex International Hotel 31–35 Grass-market ☏0845/608 3456, ⊛www .apexhotels.co.uk. This ex-university building turned 171-room business-ori-ented hotel has better-than-average rooms, some with views of the Castle. Faces the happening Grassmarket. Doubles from £90.

Edinburgh City Hotel 79 Lauriston Place ☏0131/622 7979, ⊛www .bestwesternedinburghcity.co.uk. Located near Tollcross and the Meadows, this former maternity hospital is now a reasonably individual and smartish medium-sized hotel. Doubles from £125, breakfast not included.

Novotel Edinburgh Centre 80 Lauriston Place ☏0131/656 3500, ⊛www .accorhotels.com. One of Edinburgh's more stylishly designed chain hotels; not far from the Grassmarket and theatre district, and with a small gym, indoor pool, bar and restaurant. Doubles from £129, breakfast not included.

Point Hotel 34–59 Bread St ☏0131/221 5555, ⊛www.point-hotel.co.uk. Treated to a radical contemporary makeover, this former department store is now one of Edinburgh's most individual, design-led modern hotels. There's a popular cocktail bar and a decent restaurant at street level. Doubles from £100, breakfast not included.

Sheraton Grand 1 Festival Square ☏0131/229 9131, ⊛www.sheraton .com/grandedinburgh. Modern, upmarket hotel notable for its sandstone and glass facade which looks across an open plaza to the castle, and the fact that it's home to the city's best spa (⊛www.one-spa.com) – you don't have to be resident to make use of it. Doubles from £170, breakfast not included.

Tailors Hall Hotel 139 Cowgate ☏0131/622 6801, ⊛www.festival-inns .co.uk. Stylish and modern en-suite rooms in a converted 1621 trades hall and brewery in otherwise dingy Cowgate. It's in the same building as the lively, late-night mock-Gothic *Three Sisters Bar* (and beer garden). Doubles from £80.

Along Princes Street

Balmoral Hotel 1 Princes St ☎0131/556 2414, ⊛www.roccofortehotels.com. This elegant Edinburgh landmark is the finest grand hotel in the city, with nearly two hundred rooms, full business facilities, a swimming pool and gym and two highly rated restaurants. Doubles from £290, breakfast not included.

Caledonian Hilton Hotel Corner of Princes St and Lothian Rd ☎0131/222 8888, ⊛www.hilton.co.uk. This redsandstone building lording it over the west end of Princes St and the sometimes noisy Lothian Rd, offers picture postcard views of the castle from some rooms, as well as a gym, heated pool, spa and bar. Doubles from £155.

Hudson Hotel 7–11 Hope St ☎0131/247 7000, ⊛www.thehudsonhotel.co.uk. Well-located boutique hotel behind Princes St, with contemporary, New York- inspired design throughout, plus a coffee bar, restaurant and small underground nightclub. Doubles from £150.

Old Waverley Hotel 43 Princes St ☎0131/556 4648, ⊛www.oldwaverley .co.uk. This rather old-fashioned and plain grand hotel, ideally placed right across from Waverley Station, has been recently refurbished and offers a bar and restaurant with sweeping city views. Doubles from £160.

The New Town

Ardenlee Guest House 9 Eyre Place ☎0131/556 2838, ⊛www .ardenleeguesthouse.com. Welcoming nonsmoking guesthouse at the foot of the New Town, with original Victorian features and nine reasonably spacious rooms, including some suitable for families. Doubles from £57.

Castle View Guest House 30 Castle St ☎0131/226 5784, ⊛www.castleviewgh .co.uk. A lot of stairs (and no lift), and the castle view is sideways-on (and only from certain rooms), but the eight en-suite rooms are pleasant and include some familyfriendly ones, while the location is central,

right in the heart of the New Town's shops and restaurants. Doubles from £90.

Christopher North House Hotel 6 Gloucester Place ☎0131/225 2720, ⊛www.christophernorth.co.uk. Elegant and comfortable townhouse hotel in a typically grand New Town terrace. Decor is modern and dramatic, if a little overwhelming. Doubles from £98.

Davenport House 58 Great King St ☎0131/558 8495, ⊛www .davenport-house.com. This grand, regally decorated guesthouse in an attractive townhouse makes a well-priced and intimate alternative to some of the nearby hotels. Doubles from £95.

Gerald's Place 21b Abercromby Place ☎0131/558 7017, ⊛www.geraldsplace .com. A real taste of cultured New Town life at an upmarket but wonderfully hospitable and comfy basement B&B. Doubles from £99.

7 Gloucester Place 7 Gloucester Place ☎0131/225 2974, ⊛www .stayinginscotland.com. Elegant, wellcared-for bed and breakfast, with three bedrooms on the upper floor of a Georgian terrace house. The best of the double rooms has graceful garden views and use of a classic 1930s bathroom. Doubles from £80.

Howard Hotel 34 Great King St ☎0131/557 3500, ⊛www.thehoward .com. Top-of-the-range yet discreet townhouse hotel, with eighteen exclusive rooms lavishly decorated in grand and refined style. Doubles from £165.

11 Moray Place 11 Moray Place ☎0131/226 4997, ⊛www.morayplace .co.uk. An old-fashioned B&B on a street that ranks as the finest of the New Town's architectural splendours. Rooms are on the upper floors and look either over Moray Place gardens or north to Fife. Doubles from £130.

Rick's Restaurant with Rooms 55a Frederick St ☎0131/622 7800, ⊛www .ricksedinburgh.co.uk. The ten muchsought-after rooms at the back of this popular bar and restaurant have recently been revamped with luxury wallpaper, fresh artwork and plasma screens, and look out onto a cobbled lane and courtyard behind. Doubles from £129.

ACCOMMODATION

Ardmor House	6	Express by Holiday Inn		MW Guest House	17
Argyle		Edinburgh Waterfront	3	The Original Raj Hotel	12
Backpackers Hotel	15	Fraoch House	7	Orocco Pier	8
Ashdene House	19	Globetrotter Inn	2	The Port Inn	5
Belford Hostel	11	The Greenhouse	16	Prestonfield	18
Cluaran House	14	Harbour Apartments	1	University of	
Dakota Forthbridge	10	Hawthorne House	9	Edinburgh Pollock	
Dalhousie Castle	20	Malmaison	4	Halls of Residence	13

© Crown copyright

Royal Garden Apartments York Buildings, Queen St ☏0131/625 2345, ⓦwww.royal-garden.co.uk. Superbly equipped, comfortable modern one- and two-bedroom serviced apartments very centrally located opposite the National Portrait Gallery. From £155.

Tigerlily 125 George St ☏0131 225 5005, ⓦwww.tigerlilyedinburgh.co.uk. A hip boutique hotel, bar and restaurant that epitomizes the new "Gorgeous" George St. A classic Georgian townhouse transformed into a flamboyant design extravaganza; indulgent pink or black bedroom suites are kitted out with hi-tech gadgets and decadent fabrics. Doubles from £175.

Calton Hill and Broughton

Ardmor House 74 Pilrig St, Pilrig ☏0131/554 4944, ⓦwww.ardmorhouse.com. Victorian townhouse with some lovely original features combined with smart contemporary decor. Gay-owned, straight-friendly, and located halfway between town and Leith. Doubles from £75.

Express by Holiday Inn Picardy Place, Broughton ☏0131/558 2300, ⓦwww.hieedinburgh.co.uk. A great location in an elegant old Georgian tenement near the top of Broughton St, with 161 rooms featuring neat but predictable chain-hotel decor and facilities. Doubles from £95.

Fraoch House 66 Pilrig St, Pilrig ☏0131/554 1353, ⓦwww.fraochhouse.com. A relaxing six-bedroom guesthouse with a slick, modern look created by its young owners. It's a ten- to fifteen-minute walk from both Broughton St and the heart of Leith. Doubles from £80.

The Glasshouse Hotel 2 Greenside Place, Broughton ☏0131/525 8200, ⓦwww.theetoncollection.com. Cloistered behind the castellated facade of Lady Glenorchy's Church, offering 65 chi-chi rooms with push-button curtains and sliding doors opening onto a huge, lush roof garden scattered with Philippe Starck furniture. Perfect if you're in town for a weekend of flash indulgence. Doubles from £180.

Ramsays Bed and Breakfast 25 East London St, Broughton ☏0131 557 5917, ⓦwww.ramsaysbedandbreakfastedinburgh.com. Well located just around the corner from Broughton St, this terraced townhouse has four simple and neat bedrooms, all with en-suite bathrooms. Full Scottish breakfast is served and families are welcome. Doubles from £75.

Regent House Hotel 3 Forth St, Broughton ☏0131/556 1616, ⓦwww.regenthousehotel.co.uk. A small hotel over four floors which makes up for its lack of glamour with a great location (right in the heart of Broughton on a quiet side-street), and by its practicality, with a number of the rooms useful for groups of 3–5 people. Doubles from £75; large rooms from £40 per person.

Along the Water of Leith

Canon Court Apartments 20 Canonmills ☏0131/474 7000, ⓦwww.canoncourt.co.uk. A block of smart, comfortable self-catering one- and two-bedroom apartments not far from Canonmills Bridge over the Water of Leith at the northern edge of the New Town. Studio apartments from £74 per night.

Galloway Guest House 22 Dean Park Crescent, Stockbridge ☏0131/332 3672, ⓔgalloway_theclarks@hotmail.com. Friendly family-run option in elegant Stockbridge, within walking distance of the centre. Traditional in style but neat and well priced. Doubles from £55.

Inverleith Hotel 5 Inverleith Terrace, Inverleith ☏0131/556 2745, ⓦwww.inverleithhotel.co.uk. Pleasant option near the Botanic Garden, with twelve rooms of various sizes in a Victorian terraced house; all are en suite and tastefully decorated with wooden floors, antiques and tapestries. Doubles from £89.

Six Mary's Place Raeburn Place, Stockbridge ☏0131/332 8965, ⓦwww.sixmarysplace.co.uk. A collectively run alternative-style guesthouse with eight smart, fresh-looking rooms; a no-smoking policy, and excellent home-cooked vegetarian breakfasts served in a sunny conservatory. Doubles from £80.

Leith

Express by Holiday Inn Edinburgh Waterfront Britannia Way, Ocean Drive ☏0131/555 4422, ⊛www.hiexpress .co.uk. Purpose-built budget hotel that's a good mid-price option in the Leith area. It's in walking distance of the best of the local restaurants, and the Ocean Terminal shopping centre, and an easy bus ride into town. Doubles from £89.

Harbour Apartments Western Harbour ☏0131/240 0080 ⊛www .scottishapartment.com. Part of a large modern development on the waterfront, these serviced two-bedroom apartments can be used as twins or doubles to sleep up to six. Guests get complimentary use of a nearby gym and spa and a free shuttle bus into the centre. From £69 per night.

Malmaison 1 Tower Place ☏0131/468 5000, ⊛www.malmaison.com. Chic, modern hotel set in the grand old Seamen's Hostel just back from the wharfside. Bright, bold original designs in each room, as well as CD players and cable TV. Also has gym, room service, Parisian brasserie and café-bar. Doubles from £99.

The Port Inn 48–50 Constitution St ☏0131/467 1807, ⊛www.portinn.co.uk. Stylish, minimalist rooms above a beer garden. A quieter sister bar to the neighbouring Port O Leith, featuring art exhibitions and serving home-cooked evening meals on request. Doubles from £50.

North and west Edinburgh

Bonham Hotel 35 Drumsheugh Gardens, West End ☏0131/623 9301, ⊛www .thebonham.com. One of Edinburgh's most stylish modern boutique hotels, cheekily hiding behind a grand West End Victorian facade and offering an interesting mix of fine period and chic contemporary styling throughout. Doubles from £140.

Melvin House Hotel 3 Rothesay Terrace, West End ☏0131/225 5084, ⊛www .melvinhouse.co.uk. One of Edinburgh's grandest Victorian terraced houses, with exquisite internal wood panelling and a galleried library. The rooms are rather less memorable, though some have outstanding views over Dean village and the city skyline. Doubles from £99.

The Original Raj Hotel 6 West Coates, Haymarket ☏0131/346 1333, ⊛www .rajempire.com. Imaginatively conceived and pleasantly executed, this townhouse hotel has seventeen rooms themed on India and the splendour of the Raj. Doubles from £75.

Premier Travel Inn Edinburgh City Centre 1 Morrison Link, Haymarket ☏0870/238 3319, ⊛www.travelinn .co.uk. No-frills chain hotel in a fairly mundane location near Haymarket Station, about fifteen minutes' walk from Princes St. Doubles from £69, breakfast not included.

South Edinburgh

Ashdene House 23 Fountainhall Rd, Grange ☏0131/667 6026, ⊛www .ashdenehouse.com. Well-run, environmentally friendly, non-smoking guesthouse in traditional Victorian style, located in the quiet southern suburbs. Doubles from £75.

Bruntsfield Hotel 69 Bruntsfield Place, Bruntsfield ☏0131/229 1393, ⊛www .thebruntsfield.co.uk. Large, comfortable and fairly peaceful hotel, now part of the Best Western group, a mile south of Princes St overlooking Bruntsfield Links. Doubles from £180.

Cluaran House 47 Leamington Terrace, Viewforth ☏0131/221 0047, ⊛www .cluaran-house-edinburgh.co.uk. Pleasant non-smoking B&B in a tastefully decorated house with lots of original paintings on the walls. Serves good wholefood breakfasts. Doubles from £70.

Dalhousie Castle Bonnyrigg, Midlothian ☏01875/820153, ⊛www.dalhousiecastle .co.uk. If you want a stay in a romantic Scottish castle, this is it. Located in rolling countryside about twenty minutes' drive south of the city centre, you'll find luxurious rooms, four-poster beds, log fires, suits of armour and a modern spa behind the thirteenth-century stone walls. Double rooms from £155 in a separate lodge, or £220 in the castle.

The Greenhouse 14 Hartington Gardens, Viewforth ☎0131/622 7634, ⓦwww .greenhouse-edinburgh.com. A fully vegetarian/vegan guesthouse, right down to the soaps and duvets, though a relaxed rather than right-on atmosphere prevails. The rooms are neat and tastefully furnished, with fresh fruit and flowers in each. Doubles from £70.

MW Guest House 94 Dalkeith Rd, Newington ☎0131/662 9265, ⓦwww .mwguesthouse.co.uk. One of only a few guesthouses in town with fresh, contemporary design. As it's set in a Victorian villa, every room is a bit different: those at the back are a bit quieter. If you're in a car the parking here is easier than some other Southside choices. Doubles from £70.

Prestonfield Priestfield Rd, Prestonfield ☎0131/225 7800, ⓦwww.prestonfield .com. This seventeenth-century mansion set in its own park below Arthur's Seat was recently taken over by the *Witchery* team (see p.000), and an extravagant baroque makeover has helped make it one of Edinburgh's most lavish and over-the-top places to stay. Doubles from £195.

Ten Hill Place Hotel 10 Hill Place ☎0131/662 2080, ⓦwww.tenhillplace .com. A newly opened hotel on the centrally located campus of the historic Royal College of Surgeons, with 78 sleek and smartly styled bedrooms, all run according to an environmentally conscious policy. There is no restaurant, but a breakfast buffet, room service and bar snacks are available. Doubles from £122.

South Queensferry

Dakota Forthbridge Ferrymuir Retail Park ☎0870/423 4293, ⓦwww .dakotaforthbridge.co.uk. Rather uninspiring location right beside the streams of traffic on the Forth Road Bridge, but an undoubtedly stylish yet keenly priced new hotel chain from Malmaison founder Ken McCulloch. Doubles from £89.

Hawthorne House 15 West Terrace ☎0131/319 1447, ⓦwww .hawthorne-house.com. Simple B&B in a tall, narrow house in the old part of town; the four double or family rooms are all en suite, and there's a view of the sea and bridges from those at the front, and of the pantile roofs of old South Queensferry from the rear-facing windows. Doubles from £60.

Orocco Pier 17 High St ☎0131/331 1298, ⓦwww.oroccopier.co.uk. An exciting and stylish alternative to the city centre, set in a historic house on the South Queensferry waterfront. Twelve flash rooms with designer furnishings, cool lighting and electronic mod cons, as well as a stylish bar and brasserie on site; all have great views out to the Forth Bridges. Doubles from £120.

Hostels

Edinburgh is one of the UK's most popular backpacker destinations, and there are a large number of hostels in and around the city centre, ranging in size, atmosphere and quality. Competition is fierce, so be prepared for a bit of enthusiastic marketing when you make an enquiry. For hostels, we provide the standard price of a dorm bed in regular high season, as well as the cost of a private (double or twin) room, where available. You may have to pay a little more for a dorm with fewer beds.

Argyle Backpackers Hotel 14 Argyle Place, Marchmont ☎0131/667 9991, ⓦwww.argyle-backpackers.com. Quiet, less intense version of the typical backpackers' hostel, pleasantly located in three adjoining townhouses near the

Meadows in studenty Marchmont. The small dorms have single beds, and there's a dozen or so double/twin rooms, as well as a pleasant communal conservatory and garden at the back. Dorms £12, doubles £37.

Belford Hostel 6–8 Douglas Gardens, West End ☎0131/220 2200, ⓦwww .hoppo.com. Hoppo chain hostel housed in a converted Arts and Crafts church just west of the centre, close to the Water of Leith and the Gallery of Modern Art. Dorms are in box rooms with the vaulted church ceiling above; there's also a handful of doubles. The basement communal areas are reasonably varied and spacious. Dorms £16.50, doubles £52.

Brodies 1 12 High St, Royal Mile ☎0131/556 6770, ⓦwww.brodieshostels .co.uk. Tucked down a typical Old Town close, with four fairly straightforward dorms and limited communal areas. It's smaller than many hostels, and a little bit more homely as a result. Dorms £11.

Brodies 2 93 High St, Royal Mile ☎0131/556 2223, ⓦwww.brodieshostels .co.uk. The mellow atmosphere at this smart new hostel is even more marked than in the sister property across the road. Smaller dorms as well as doubles and triples. Dorms £11, doubles £44.

Castle Rock Hostel 15 Johnston Terrace, Old Town ☎0131/225 9666, ⓦwww.castlerockedinburgh.com. Tucked below the castle ramparts, with 200 or so beds arranged in large, bright dorms, as well as triple and quad rooms and some doubles. The communal areas include a games room with pool and ping-pong tables. Dorms £14, triple and quad rooms £17, doubles £45.

Cowgate Tourist Hostel 94–116 Cowgate, Old Town ☎0131/226 2153, ⓦwww.hostelsaccommodation.com. Basic but central accommodation in small three-four-and five-bedroom apartments with kitchens, all in the heart of the Old Town. Single bed in apartment £12, twin rooms £40.

Edinburgh Backpackers Hostel 65 Cockburn St, Old Town ☎0131/220 2200, ⓦwww.hoppo.com. Very central, with large but bright dorms and a decent number of doubles in a tall Old Town building. The communal areas are pretty standard, though there is a bar and café at street level. Dorms £11, doubles £30.

Edinburgh Central SYHA 9 Haddington Place, Leith ☎0870/155 3255, ⓦwww .edinburghcentral.org. In a handy location at the top of Leith Walk, this five-star hostel has single, double and 8-bed rooms with en-suite facilities. There is a reasonably priced bistro or self-catering kitchen facilities. Singles from £15, twins from £37, family rooms from £67.

Eglinton SYHA Hostel 18 Eglinton Crescent, Haymarket ☎0870/004 1116, ⓦwww.syha.org.uk. Situated in a characterful townhouse west of the centre, and popular with groups and families. Dorms are large, and the communal areas can be overrun by groups. Non-smoking, and Internet access available. Dorms £14.50.

Globetrotter Inn 46 Marine Drive, Cramond ☎0131/336 1030, ⓦwww .globetrotterinns.com. A big departure from the busy, buzzy city-centre hostels, in a sylvan parkland setting four miles from the centre with lovely views of the Firth of Forth. The 350-plus beds are mostly bunks with privacy curtains and individual reading lights, but there are also doubles. There's access to a gym and sauna, lots of parking and an hourly shuttle service into town, as well as regular buses (#42). Families and kids are not encouraged. Dorms £15, doubles £46.

High Street Hostel 8 Blackfriars St, Old Town ☎0131/557 3984, ⓦwww .highstreethostel.com. Lively and popular hostel in an attractive sixteenth-century building just off the Royal Mile. There are only dorms here, but good communal facilities, which are shared by those staying at the *Royal Mile Backpackers* just up the road. Dorms £14.

Royal Mile Backpackers 105 High St, Old Town ☎0131/557 6120, ⓦwww .royalmilebackpackers.com. Smallish hostel popular with longer-term residents. The communal areas here are very limited, but guests have use of the facilities in nearby sister hostels. Dorms £14.

Smart City Hostel 50 Blackfriars St, Old Town ☎0131/452 9079, ⓦwww .smartcityhostels.com. A five-star hostel just off the Royal Mile, with 620 beds in twin rooms or dorms. Girls- only rooms are also available. A simple buffet serves good value pub food and breakfasts and there is a late night bar for residents. Dorm beds from £18.

St Christopher's Inn **9–13 Market St, Old Town** ☎**0131/226 1446,** ⊛**www .st-christophers.co.uk.** Huge and a little corporate but very much in the modern hostel style – dorms are of varying size and have en-suite bathrooms; some have TVs and there are a few double rooms. There's a small communal area but no kitchen; the ground-floor bar serves food, though it has more of a reputation for its noisy party atmosphere and screenings of antipodean rugby games. Dorms from £14, doubles £48.

Essentials

Arrival and getting around

Edinburgh International Airport (℡ 0870/040 0007, ⊛ www.baa.com) is at Turnhouse, seven miles west of the city centre close to the start of the M8 motorway to Glasgow. Airlink shuttle buses (#100) connect to Waverley railway station in the centre of town in just under half an hour; they run 24 hours a day, with services departing every ten or twenty minutes between 5am and midnight, then hourly through the night (£3 single). Lothian Bus #35 (daytime only every 20–30min; £1) runs from the airport to the west of Edinburgh, the Royal Mile and Leith, but takes significantly longer. Taxis charge £15–20 from the airport into the town centre. Edinburgh Shuttle (℡ 0845/500 5000; ⊛ www.edinburghshuttle.com) operates a frequent shared taxi service using seven-seater mini-buses and runs between the airport and any address in a large chunk of central Edinburgh for £8 for a single journey.

Situated right at the heart of the city between Princes Street and the Royal Mile, **Waverley Station** (℡ 0845/748 4950, ⊛ www.nationalrail.co.uk) is the terminus for all mainline trains. Most services from England are run by GNER (℡ 0845/722 5225, ⊛ www.gner.co.uk) or Virgin Trains (℡ 0845/722 2333, ⊛ www.virgintrains .co.uk); sleeper services from London and all services within Scotland are operated by First Scotrail (℡ 0845/755 0033, ⊛ www.scotrail.co.uk). There's a rank for black taxis within the station, while buses to all parts of town leave from the adjacent streets. There's a second mainline train stop, **Haymarket Station**, just under two miles west on the lines from Waverley to Glasgow, Fife and the Highlands, although this is only really of use if you're staying nearby.

The **coach** terminal for local and inter-city services is on St Andrew Square, two minutes' walk from Waverley Station on the opposite side of Princes Street.

Run by Superfast (℡ 0870/234 0870, ⊛ www.superfast.com), **ferries** cross from Zeebrugge in Belgium to Rosyth, not far from the Forth Road Bridge to the north-west of Edinburgh, three times each week. Bus #X2 runs into town from here (£3).

City transport

Although Edinburgh occupies a large area relative to its population, most places worth visiting lie within the compact city centre, which is easily explored on foot. To get to the suburbs, however, or to travel across the central area, the local **public transport** system is a relatively simple and efficient option, with most services terminating on or near Princes Street. The city is generally well served by **buses**; most useful are the white and maroon ones operated by **Lothian Buses** (⊛ www.lothianbuses .co.uk), which provide the most frequent and comprehensive coverage of the city. Usefully, every bus stop displays diagrams indicating which services pass the stop and which routes they take. Lothian Buses timetables and passes are available from their ticket centres on Waverley Bridge, Shandwick Place or 27 Hanover St (enquiry line ℡ 0131/555 6363). A good investment, especially if you're staying away from the centre or want to explore the suburbs, is the £13 "Ridacard" bus pass allowing a week's unlimited travel on Lothian services; Lothian also offer a LRT day pass allowing unlimited travel for £2.50. Tickets are also available from drivers; you'll need exact change, and the most common fare is £1. The predominantly white buses of **First Edinburgh** (℡ 0870/872 7271; ⊛ www .firstgroup.com) also cover a number of the main routes through town, but are better for outlying towns and villages. They have their own system of tickets and day-tickets, similar in structure to Lothian Buses: for travel within the city, the standard fare is £1, with unlimited day travel for £2.30. Most services depart from and terminate at or near St Andrew Square, where the main **bus and coach station** is located, or Waterloo Place, the eastern extension of Princes Street.

The city is well endowed with **taxi** ranks, and you can also hail black cabs on the street. Costs are reasonable – you'll pay around £6 from the city centre to Leith, for example. If you want to call a taxi, try one of the following; Computer Cabs ☎0131/228 2555; Central Radio Taxis ☎0131/229 2468; or City Cabs ☎0131/228 1211.

Edinburgh has almost no suburban **rail** services; the one main place of interest served by trains is South Queensferry, with all mainline services to Fife, Inverness and Aberdeen stopping at Dalmeny Station (see p.149).

Tours

Open-top **bus tours** are big business in Edinburgh, with four rival companies taking largely similar routes around the main sights. All depart from Waverley Bridge and all allow you to get on and off at leisure. The most entertaining of the four are MacTours (☎0131/556 2244, ☎www.mactours.co.uk), which use a fleet of characterful vintage buses. Most of the **walking tours** are based on and around the Royal Mile; for more on these, see p.66. Elsewhere in the city, Geowalks (☎0131/555 5488, ☎www.geowalks.demon.co.uk), offers guided walks up Arthur's Seat in the company of a qualified geologist; Rebustours (☎07866/536752, ☎www .rebustours.com) trace the footsteps of Inspector Rebus, hero of Ian Rankin's bestselling detective novels; while the city tours offered by Leith Walks (☎0131/555 2500, ☎www.leithwalks .co.uk) include a *Trainspotting* tour of some of the scenes famous from Irvine Welsh's novels. Adrian's Edinburgh City Cycle Tour (☎07966/477206, ☎www.edinburghcycletour.com) uses pedal-power for an enjoyable and good-value three-hour Edinburgh tour, with all equipment provided. If you want a break from the city, Walkabout Scotland (☎0845/686 1344, ☎www .walkaboutscotland.com) will pick you up from the city centre and whisk you off on a one-day walking trip in the Highlands.

Prices range from £7–8 for walking tours to £15 for the cycle tour and £50 for a Walkabout Scotland day-trip.

Information

Edinburgh's main **tourist office** is on top of Princes Mall near the northern entrance to Waverley Station (April & Oct Mon–Sat 9am–6pm, Sun 10am–6pm; May, June & Sept Mon–Sat 9am–7pm, Sun 10am–7pm; July & Aug Mon–Sat 9am–8pm, Sun 10am–8pm; Nov–March Mon–Wed 9am–5pm, Thurs–Sat 9am–6pm, Sun 10am–5pm; ☎0845/225 5121, ☎www.edinburgh .org). Although inevitably hectic at the height of the season, it's reasonably efficient, with scores of free leaflets and a bank of computers available if you want to search for information on the web (£1 for 20mins). The much smaller **airport branch** is in the main concourse, directly opposite Gate 5 (daily: April–Oct 6.30am–10.30pm; Nov–March 7am–9pm).

The best guide to local events is *The List* (£2.20), available fortnightly from newsagents; more suggestions for finding out what's on are given opposite.

Websites

ⓦ www.edinburgh.org Edinburgh and Lothian tourist board site, with a wealth of local info and an online accommodation booking service.

ⓦ www.edinburgh.gov.uk This Edinburgh City Council site gives the lowdown on local services, from transport to kids' facilities, and has lots of links.

ⓦ www.edinburghfestivals.co.uk A good gateway into all Edinburgh's major festivals, including the Fringe, Film Festival and Hogmanay.

ⓦ www.scotsman.com News site for the main local daily newspaper and *Edinburgh Evening News*.

ⓦ www.list.co.uk Entertainment and events guide to Edinburgh and Glasgow, with good coverage of cinema, theatre, music and art, as well as eating out.

ⓦ www.theoracle.co.uk Straightforward but useful what's-on site with comprehensive listings.

ⓦ www.edinburghguide.com Good links directory covering everything from entertainment to education; decent listings for theatre and cinema, too.

ⓦ www.kidsedinburgh.com Searchable database that offers ideas and suggestions for places to visit and events for different age groups.

ⓦ www.edinburgh-galleries.co.uk This well-maintained site details exhibitions taking place at most of Edinburgh's public and private galleries.

ⓦ www.edinburgharchitecture.co.uk Attractive site dedicated to the capital's contemporary architecture and design, with photos, suggested tours and details of the coolest restaurants and hotels.

ⓦ www.ceolas.org Site specializing in Celtic music, both historical and contemporary, with lots of tunes to listen to.

ⓦ www.origins.net A good place to start searching for your long-lost Scottish ancestors, developed in association with the General Register Office of Scotland.

ⓦ www.geo.ed.ac.uk Follow the links to "Web Resources" and then to "Gateway to Scotland" for some excellent background information to all things Scottish, and a myriad of links.

ⓦ www.rampantscotland.com Excellent links directory, organized by subject, covering all aspects of Scotland.

Entertainment

Inevitably, Edinburgh's entertainment scene is at its best during the Festival (see p.176), which can make the other 49 weeks of the year seem like a bit of an anticlimax. The city does have plenty to offer throughout the year, however, especially in the realm of theatre and music.

The best way to **find out what's on** is to pick up a copy of *The List* (see opposite). Alternatively, get hold of the *Edinburgh Evening News* (Mon–Sat): its listings column gives details of performances in the city that day, including those at hotels and bars. For information on nightclubs, you can also check out the posters and piles of flyers distributed to most of the pre-club bars around town. Box offices of individual halls and theatres are likewise liberally supplied with promotional leaflets about forthcoming music and theatre, and some are able to sell tickets for more than one venue.

Nightclubs

The Bongo Club 37 Holyrood Rd, Old Town ☏0131/558 7604, ⓦwww .thebongoclub.co.uk. Daily till 3am. Legendary Edinburgh club that attracts some of the most interesting DJs around. Look out for the mighty Messenger Sound System pumping out reggae twice-monthly on Saturdays.

Cabaret Voltaire 36–38 Blair St, Old Town ☏0131/220 6176, ⓦwww .thecabaretvoltaire.com. Daily 10.30pm–3am. A nightclub in the atmospheric setting of the Old Town's underground vaults. The venue plays host to some of the city's best clubs such as deep-house favourite Ultragroove and Taste, an evening of frenetic hard-house that has long been a favourite with the city's gay community.

Citrus Club 40–42 Grindlay St, West End ☏0131/6227086, ⓦwww.citrusclub .co.uk. Thurs–Sat 10.30pm–3am. A real Edinburgh perennial, this club is frequented by a mixed crowd, comprising everyone from students to professionals, and serves up an unchallenging but enjoyable blend of indie and eighties classics.

Ego 14 Picardy Place, Broughton ℡0131/478 7434, ⊕www.clubego .co.uk. Tues–Sat 11pm–3am, Sun & Mon reserved for private parties/special events. A former casino, this big venue is the monthly home for acclaimed Glasgow club Optimo and the epic party night Vegas. The smaller *Cocteau Lounge* downstairs is occasionally in use for more intimate alternative and retro club nights.

The Liquid Room 9c Victoria St, Old Town ℡0131/225 2564, ⊕www.liquidroom .com. Tues–Sun 10.30pm–3am. One of the best of Edinburgh's larger venues, with nights such as the indie Evol, and Luvely, a popular gay-friendly house night.

Opal Lounge 51 George St, New Town ℡0131/226 2275, ⊕www.opallounge .co.uk. Daily noon–3am. See and be-seen bar in the New Town with DJs funk-ing things up later on. As well as the beautiful people you'll also find office groups lingering on long after their post-work drink.

Gay clubs and bars

CC Blooms 23 Greenside Place, Broughton ℡0131/556 9331. Daily 6pm–3am. Edinburgh's only uniquely gay club, with a big dancefloor, stonking rhythms and a young, friendly crowd.

Planet Out 6 Baxter's Place, Broughton ℡0131/524 0061. Mon–Fri 5pm–1am. Sun 12.30pm–1am. This loud and outra-geous bar beside the Playhouse Theatre operates mostly as a pre-club venue, but it's a popular drinking spot in its own right and is known as *the* place to meet people.

Sala Café Bar 60 Broughton St, Broughton ℡0131/478 7069, ⊕www .salacafe.co.uk. Mon–Thurs & Sun 11am–11pm, Fri & Sat 11am–1am. Bar food, light snacks and drinks in a relaxed atmosphere at the Edinburgh Gay, Lesbian and Bisexual Centre.

Live music venues

Bannermans 212 Cowgate, Old Town ℡0131/556 3254, ⊕www .bannermansgigs.co.uk. Daily mid-day–1am. This longstanding pub is the best place in central Edinburgh to discover local indie bands hoping for a big break, with live music every evening but Tuesday.

The Bongo Club 37 Holyrood Rd, Old Town ℡0131/558 7604, ⊕www .thebongoclub.co.uk. A smashing sound system and a relaxed atmosphere makes this one of the city's best places to catch local alternative acts playing live but name artists also make regular appearances.

Corn Exchange 11 Newmarket Rd, Slateford ℡0131/477 3500, ⊕www .ece.uk.com. This rather misleadingly named former slaughterhouse is now a popular 3000-capacity venue for big-name contemporary pop and rock acts, but the location, three miles west of the centre, is a bit off-putting.

Jazz Centre@The Lot 4–6 Grassmarket; ℡0131/467 5200. Wed–Sat 8–11pm. Edinburgh's premier jazz venue, with live music from top local and national performers.

The Liquid Room 9c Victoria St, Old Town ℡0131/225 2564, ⊕www .liquidroom.com. Closed Mon. One of Edinburgh's best mid-sized venues for touring indie and R&B bands; gigs are interspersed with club nights.

Royal Oak 1 Infirmary St, Old Town ℡0131/557 2976, ⊕www .royal-oak-folk.com. Mon–Sat 11am–2am, Sun 12.30pm–2am. A traditional pub hosting regular informal folk sessions and the "Wee Folk Club", featuring gigs by guest performers on Sundays.

Queen's Hall 89 Clerk St, Newington ℡0131/668 2019, ⊕www.thequeenshall .net. Converted Georgian church which now operates as a concert hall; it's used prin-cipally by the Scottish Chamber Orchestra and Scottish Ensemble, as well as touring jazz, blues and folk groups.

Sandy Bell's 25 Forrest Rd, Old Town ℡0131/225 2751. Mon–Sat 11.30am–1am, Sun 12.30–11pm. This friendly bar is a good bet for folk music most nights of the week.

Usher Hall Corner of Lothian Rd and Grindlay St, West End ℡0131/228 1155, ⊕www.usherhall.co.uk. Edinburgh's main civic concert hall, seating over 2500, is excellent for choral and symphony con-certs, but less suitable for solo vocalists. The upper circle seats are cheapest and have the best acoustics, but the sound quality overall is much improved after a recent refurbishment.

Whistlebinkies 4–6 South Bridge, Old Town ℡0131/557 5114, ⊕www .whistlebinkies.com. Daily 7pm–3am. One of Edinburgh's most reliable venues for live music every night of the week – often it's rock and pop covers, though there are some folk evenings.

Theatre and dance venues

Assembly Rooms 54 George St, New Town ☎0131/623 3030, ⊛www .assemblyrooms.com. This venerable complex of small and large halls is used all year, but really comes into its own during the Fringe, when large-scale drama productions and mainstream comedy are staged. At other times it's used for shows, dances and the occasional music event.

Dance Base 14–16 Grassmarket, Old Town ☎0131/225 5255, ⊛www .dancebase.co.uk. Scotland's sparkling new National Centre for Dance is used mostly for modern dance workshops and classes, but also hosts occasional performances.

Festival Theatre Nicolson St, Old Town ☎0131/529 6000, ⊛www.eft.co.uk. Until recently the largest stage in Britain, principally used for Scottish Opera and Scottish Ballet's appearances in the capital, as well as for everything from children's shows to Engelbert Humperdinck.

King's Theatre 2 Leven St, Tollcross ☎0131/529 6000, ⊛www.eft.co.uk. Stately Edwardian civic theatre that majors in pantomime, touring West End plays and the occasional major drama or opera performance.

Playhouse Theatre 18–22 Greenside Place, Broughton ☎0870/606 3424, ⊛www.edinburgh-playhouse.co.uk. Recently refurbished, this former cinema is one of the most capacious theatres in Britain, and plays host to extended runs of popular musicals as well as occasional rock concerts.

Royal Lyceum Theatre 30 Grindlay St, West End ☎0131/248 4848, ⊛www .lyceum.org.uk. This fine Victorian civic theatre, with its compact auditorium, is Edinburgh's leading year-round venue for mainstream drama.

Theatre Workshop 34 Hamilton Place, Stockbridge ☎0131/226 5425, ⊛www .theatre-workshop.com. Enticing programme of innovative international theatre and performance art. Strong in the Festival and over Christmas, but fewer shows at other times.

Traverse Theatre 10 Cambridge St, West End ☎0131/228 1404, ⊛www.traverse .co.uk. Unquestionably one of Britain's premier venues for new plays and avant-garde drama from around the world, and going from strength to strength in its new custom-built home beside the Usher Hall.

Comedy venues

Jongleurs Omni Centre, Greenside Place, Broughton ☎0870/787 0707, ⊛www .jongleurs.com. Thurs–Sat 7pm–3am (last entry 8.30pm). This Edinburgh link in a national chain, located in a huge glass-fronted cinema complex at the foot of Calton Hill, offers a year-round chance to encounter popular Festival stand-up acts and national stars.

The Stand 5 York Place, New Town ☎0131/558 7272, ⊛www.thestand .co.uk. Mon–Sat 7.30pm–1am, Sun 12.30pm–midnight. The city's top comedy spot, with a different act on every night and some of the UK's best comics headlining at the weekends. The bar is worth a visit in itself.

Cinemas

Cameo 38 Home St, Tollcross ☎0131/228 2800, ⊛www.picturehouses .co.uk. A treasure of an arthouse cinema, screening more challenging mainstream releases alongside cult late-nighters.

Dominion 18 Newbattle Terrace, Morningside ☎0131/447 4771, ⊛www .dominioncinema.com. A reminder of how cinemas were before multiplexes, the Dominion is still family-owned, and battling on with its screenings of popular new releases.

Filmhouse 88 Lothian Rd, West End ☎0131/228 2688, ⊛www .filmhousecinema.com. Three screens showing an eclectic programme of independent, arthouse and classic films. The café is chief hangout for the city's film buffs.

Odeon 118 Lothian Rd, West End ☎0871/224 4007, ⊛www.odeon.co.uk. Central four-screen cinema showing the latest releases.

UGC Fountainpark Dundee St, Fountainbridge ☎0871/200 2000, ⊛www .ugccinemas.co.uk. Buses #1, #28, #34 & #35. Big, reasonably central multiplex not far from Tollcross and Bruntsfield.

Vue Ocean Terminal, Ocean Drive, Leith ☎0871/224 0240, ⊛www.myvue. com. Buses #1, #11, #22, #34, #35. Big multiplex in the developing docklands, with plenty of bars and restaurants nearby.

Vue Omni Centre Greenside Place, Broughton ☎0871/224 0240, ⊛www .myvue.com. Most central of Edinburgh's big new multi-screen venues, tucked under Calton Hill at the top of Leith Walk.

The Edinburgh Festival

For the best part of August, the character of Scotland's capital is completely transformed by the **Edinburgh Festival**, the world's largest celebration of the arts. Every available performance space – from the grandest concert halls to pub courtyards – plays host to a packed programme of cultural entertainment, ranging from world-class opera to student revues. The streets fill with buskers and craft stalls, and the local population swells to twice its normal size as tourists, performers, media types and festival-goers throng the city centre. Pubs and restaurants stay open later, promotional posters plaster every vertical space and the atmosphere in town takes on a surreal but energized buzz.

The Edinburgh Festival is actually an umbrella term, which encompasses different festivals taking place at around the same time in the city. The principal events are the Edinburgh International Festival and the much larger Edinburgh Festival Fringe, but there are also Book, Jazz and Blues and Television festivals, the Military Tattoo on the Castle Esplanade and the Edinburgh Mela, an Asian festival held over a weekend in late August/early September.

Doing the Festival

For the visitor, the sheer volume of the Festival's output can be bewildering: virtually every branch of arts and entertainment is represented somewhere, and world-famous stars mix with pub singers in the daily line-up. It can be a struggle to find accommodation, get hold of the tickets you want, book a table in a restaurant or simply get from one side of town to another; you can end up seeing something truly dire, or something mind-blowing; you'll inevitably try to do too much, stay out too late or spend too much money – but then again, most Festival veterans will tell you that if you don't experience these things then you haven't really done the Festival.

Dates, venues, names, star acts, happening bars and burning issues change from one year to the next. This unpredictability is one of the Festival's greatest charms, however, so while the following information will help you get to grips with it, be prepared for – indeed, enjoy – the unexpected. For up-to-the-minute information at any time of year, visit ⓦ www.edinburghfestivals.co.uk, which has links to the home pages of most of the main festivals. Each festival produces its own programme well in advance, while during the Festival various publications give information about what's on day-by-day, among them *The Guide*, published daily by the Fringe Office, and local what's-on guide *The List*, which comes out weekly during the Festival and manages to combine comprehensive coverage with a reliably on-the-pulse sense of what's hot and what's not. Of the local newspapers, *The Scotsman* carries a dedicated daily Festival supplement with an events diary and reviews which carry a lot of weight, while *The Herald*, published in Glasgow, and the London-based papers offer more selective but generally authoritative reviews. Various freebie newspapers are also available around town – best of these is *Fest*, which mixes news with pithy reviews and yet more listings.

The Edinburgh International Festival

The **Edinburgh International Festival** (sometimes called the "Official Festival") was the original Edinburgh Festival, conceived in 1947 as a celebration of pan-European culture in the post-war era. Initially dominated by opera, other elements such as top-grade theatre, ballet, dance and classical music were gradually introduced, and it's still very much a highbrow event, with forays into populist territory rare. The festival generally runs over the second two weeks of August and the first week of September, and attracts truly international stars alongside some of the world's finest orchestras and opera, theatre and ballet companies. The most popular single event is the dramatic **Fireworks Concert**, held late at night on the final Sunday: the Scottish Chamber Orchestra belts out pop classics from the Ross Bandstand in Princes Street Gardens, accompanied by a spectacular pyrotechnic display high up above the ramparts of the castle. Unless you want a seat right by the orchestra you don't need a ticket for this event: hundreds of thousands of people view the display from various vantage points throughout the city, the prime spots being Princes Street, Northbridge, Calton Hill or Inverleith Park and the Botanic Gardens by Stockbridge.

Otherwise, **performances** take place at the city's larger venues such as the Usher Hall and the Festival Theatre and, while **ticket prices** run to over £40, it is possible to see shows for £10 or less if you're prepared to queue for the handful of seats sold on the day. The International Festival's headquarters are at The Hub (see p.67); you can contact them for further information, including the annual programme, which is released in April.

The Edinburgh Festival Fringe

Even standing alone from its sister festivals, the **Edinburgh Festival Fringe**, which runs over the final three weeks of August, is a monumental arts gathering – each year it sees over 15,000 performances from 700-plus companies, and features some 12,000 participants from all over the world. There are around 1500 shows every day, round the clock, in 200 venues around the city. While the headlining names at the International Festival reinforce the Festival's cultural credibility as a whole, it is the dynamism, spontaneity and sheer exuberance of the Fringe which dominates Edinburgh every August, giving the city its unique atmosphere. Crucially, because no artistic control is imposed on those who want to produce a show as part of the Fringe, the productions range from the inspired to the diabolical; there's also a highly competitive atmosphere in which one bad review in a prominent publication means box-office disaster. Many unknowns rely on self-publicity, taking to the streets to perform highlights from their show, or pressing leaflets into the hands of every passer-by.

These days, the most prominent aspect of the Fringe is **comedy**. As well as sell-out audiences and quotable reviews, most of the comedy acts are chasing the Perrier Comedy Award, given to the outstanding up-and-coming stand-up or comedy cabaret, and there's no doubt that the Edinburgh Festival is *the* place to catch new talent before it becomes famous, with debuts made by everyone from Monty Python to Graham Norton over the years. Despite the profile of comedy, however, it's still outweighed in terms of number of shows by the Fringe's **theatre** offerings, with hundreds of brand new works airing alongside offbeat classics and familiar Shakespearean tragedies. The venues are often as imaginative as the shows themselves – play-parks, restaurants and even parked cars have all been used to stage plays. The Fringe also offers fine musicals, dance, children's shows, exhibitions, lectures and music – after years of neglect the latter, in particular, has now expanded significantly, with sub-festivals and venues dedicated to youth

Fringe venues

In addition to numerous tiny and unexpected auditoriums, the four main Fringe venues are the *Assembly Rooms*, the *Pleasance*, the *Gilded Balloon* and tersely named relative newcomer, *C*. Venue complexes rather than single spaces, the latter three colonize nearby spaces for the duration of the Festival – all are safe bets for decent shows and a bit of star-spotting.

The atmosphere at the *Pleasance* is usually less frenetic than at the other venues, with classy drama and whimsical appearances by panellists on Radio 4 game shows. The *Assembly Rooms* provide a grand setting for top-of-the-range drama by companies such as the RSC and big-name music and comedy acts. The Fringe's premier comedy venue, *The Gilded Balloon*, lost its longstanding home in a fire in early 2003, but was up and running in various new venues around town by the time the Festival came along. The disparate locations of C have the most varied programme of the big four, and in recent years have been known to stage controversial productions that other venues might be too wary to promote.

While it's nothing like as large as the venues above, you shouldn't ignore the programme put on at the *Traverse Theatre*'s three stages. Long a champion of new drama, the "Trav" combines the avant-garde with slick presentation, and its plays are generally among the Fringe's most acclaimed.

orchestras, folk and roots music, as well as indie, pop and rock.

The full **Fringe programme** is usually available in June from the Festival Fringe Office (℡ 0131/226 0000, ⓦ www .edfringe.com). Postal and telephone bookings for shows can be made immediately after its release, while during the Festival, tickets are sold at the Fringe Office on the Royal Mile at no. 180 (daily 10am–9pm), as well as online or at venues. **Ticket prices** for most Fringe shows start at £5, and average from £8 to £12 at the main venues, with the better-known acts going for even more. Although some theatre and music acts can be longer, most performances are scheduled to run for an hour. Performances go on round the clock: if so inclined, you could sit through twenty shows in a day.

Edinburgh International Film Festival

In 2007, the **Edinburgh International Film Festival** took the decision to move its programme from August, where it had traditionally run alongside the International Festival and Fringe, to the second half of June, beginning with the 2008 event. One of Europe's oldest film festivals, it claims a distinguished history at the cutting edge of cinema, premiering blockbusters from directors like Steven Spielberg and Woody Allen, discovering low-budget smashes such as *My Beautiful Launderette* and the *Blair Witch Project*, and introducing serious contenders such as *East is East*, *Amelie* and *Super Size Me*.

The Film Festival offers the chance to see some of the year's more intriguing movies before they go on general release, along with a varied and exciting bill of reissues; for those in the industry, it's also a vital talking shop, with debates, seminars and workshops all spiced up by the attendance of Hollywood stars. **Tickets** (£5–10, pre-booking often necessary) and **information** are available from the main venue, the Filmhouse, 88 Lothian Rd, EH3 9BZ ℡ 0131/228 2688, ⓦ www.edfilmfest.org.uk.

Edinburgh International Book Festival

Launched in 1983, the annual two-week **Edinburgh International Book**

Festival, which takes place in the last two weeks of August, is a mammoth celebration of the written word. It's held in a tented village in the genteel setting of Charlotte Square, and offers talks, readings and signings by a star-studded line-up of visiting authors, as well as panel discussions and workshops. Well-known local writers such as Ian Rankin, A.L. Kennedy and Alexander McCall-Smith make an appearance most years, while visitors from further afield have included Doris Lessing, Louis de Bernières, Ben Okri, John Updike and Vikram Seth. In addition, there are cook-ups by celebrity chefs promoting their latest tomes, and a dedicated programme of children's activities and book-related events.

Tickets (generally £7–8) often sell out quickly, particularly for the big-name events. For tickets and info during the Festival, contact the ticket office at Charlotte Square (☎ 0131/624 5050, Ⓦ www.edbookfest.co.uk); for **information** before it starts, check the festival website or contact its administration office at 5a Charlotte Square, EH2 4DR ☎ 0131/718 5666.

Edinburgh International Jazz and Blues Festival

The **Edinburgh International Jazz and Blues Festival** runs immediately prior to the Fringe in the first week in August, easing the city into the festival spirit with a full programme of gigs in many different locations. Like all the other festivals, this one has grown over the years from a concentrated international summer camp to a bigger, more modern affair, reflecting the panoply of generations and styles which appear under the banner of jazz and blues. Scotland's own varied and vibrant jazz scene is always fully represented, and atmospheric late-night clubs complement major concerts given by international stars. Past visitors have included B.B. King, Bill Wyman, Dizzy Gillespie, Dave Brubeck, Van Morrison, Carol Kidd and the Blues Band, while

highlight events include Jazz On A Summer's Day, a musical extravaganza in Princes Street Gardens, and a colourful New Orleans-style street parade.

The **programme** is available at Ⓦ www.edinburghjazzfestival.co.uk and Ⓦ www.jazzmusic.co.uk or call ☎ 0131/467 5200. **Tickets** range in price from £5 for small pub gigs to £20 for a seat in the big venue, and are available from The Hub, Castlehill (☎ 0131/473 2000, Ⓦ www.hubtickets .co.uk).

The Military Tattoo

Staged in the spectacular stadium of the Edinburgh Castle esplanade, the **Military Tattoo** is an unashamed display of pomp and military pride. The programme of choreographed drills, massed pipe bands, historical tableaux, energetic battle re-enactments, national dancing and pyrotechnics has been a feature of the Festival for fifty years, the emotional climax provided by a lone piper on the castle battlements. Followed by a quick firework display (longer and more splendid on Saturdays), it's a successful formula barely tampered with over the years.

Tickets (£13–40 depending on seat location) are often said to be sold out months in advance, though block bookings form a large part of the sales and returns are always possible. If you're going to the show, it's advisable to take a cushion and rainwear. Both tickets and general **information** are available from the Tattoo Office, 32 Market St, EH1 1QB ☎ 0131/225 1188, Ⓦ www.edintattoo.co.uk.

The Edinburgh Mela

Held halfway between the New Town and Leith in Pilrig Park over the first weekend in September, the **Edinburgh Mela** coincides with the finale of the International Festival. Truly a people's event, it was introduced in the mid-1990s by the capital's Asian community – the word "Mela" is a Sanskrit term meaning "gathering", and is used to describe many different community events and festivals on the Asian subcontinent. In Edinburgh, the Mela is about cultural diversity, and the family-oriented programme is designed to celebrate the many different cultures in the city. Music, dance, foods, carnivals, fashion shows, sports, children's events, crafts and a two-day careers fair for school-leavers see the festival season out with a bang rather than a whimper. Further **details** are available from Edinburgh Mela, ☎ 0131/339 3583, ⓦ www.edinburgh-mela.co.uk.

Events calendar

January 1
Loony Dook South Queensferry beach. **Free.** While most of Edinburgh sleeps off its Hogmanay hangover (see opposite) a group of hardy locals and over-enthusiastic visitors go for a swim in the Firth of Forth at noon. Join in if you're brave enough, or just look on – and shiver.

January 1–31
Turner Watercolours National Gallery of Scotland (see p.101) ☎ 0131/624 6200, ⓦ www.natgalscot.ac.uk. **Free.** While the light is at its weakest, the gallery's splendid collection of watercolours by J.M.W. Turner is put on display.

January 25
Burns' Night Scots dust down their kilts to celebrate the birthday of Robert Burns, the national bard. Burns Suppers involving haggis, whisky, poetry recitations and songs are traditionally held around this date; if you don't secure an invitation, some are open to the public (check local listings/posters for details), while restaurants put on a special Burns' Night menu.

February/March
Rugby Internationals Murrayfield Stadium (see p.142) ☎ 0131/346 5000, ⓦ www.scottishrugby.org. **Average ticket price £35.** Scotland's rugby union team take on England, Wales, Ireland, France and Italy in the annual Six Nations tournament; in any year, two or three matches will be played in front of 65,000 spectators at Murrayfield Stadium.

April
Science Festival ☎ 0131/558 7666, ⓦ www.sciencefestival.co.uk. **£5–9 per event.** An increasingly high-profile and enterprising Easter festival dedicated to science and technology, offering lots of fun, hands-on events for kids and families, along with newsworthy discussion forums and more serious lectures.

30 April
Beltane Fire Festival Calton Hill (see p.114). A modern incarnation of the old Celtic festival, celebrating the arrival of spring, which takes place outdoors on the night before May Day – lots of painted naked flesh, troops of beating drums, huge bonfires and plenty of New-Agey symbolism. **Tickets cost around £5.**

Late May/early June
Children's Festival ☎ 0131/225 8050, ⓦ www.imaginate.org.uk. **Tickets from £5.** A sort of mini-Edinburgh Festival for mini folk, with a lively line-up of top-grade children's theatre, puppetry and dance from around the world held at various venues throughout town.

June
Taste of Edinburgh Meadows ⓦ www.channel4.com/tastefestivals. **From £12.** Follows a formula successful in London and other UK cities which sees top local restaurants setting up in a tented village alongside cooking theatres, taste workshops and producers' fairs, with celebrity chefs and TV tie-ins prominent.

Royal Highland Show Royal Highland Showground, Ingliston ☎ 0131/335 6200, ⓦ www.royalhighlandshow.org. **£18.** This four-day agricultural fair is Scotland's largest – prize livestock and lots of tractors dominate, but there are also food and craft halls, sheep shearing and show jumping.

Edinburgh International Film Festival Now held in late June rather than as one of the traditional August fixtures. See p.178.

July
Pride Scotia ☎ 0131/556 9471, ⓦ www.pride-scotia.org. Colourful, high-spirited

annual parade and rally staged by Scotland's lesbian, gay and transgender community. Alternates between Glasgow (even years) and Edinburgh (odd years).

Late July
Jazz and Blues Festival This week-long series of gigs and grooves gets the city in the mood for the Edinburgh Festival. See p.179.

August
Edinburgh Festival The various parts of this mind-boggling festival dominate the capital throughout August. See p.179.

Late August/early September
Edinburgh Mela ☎0131/339 3583, ⓦwww.edinburgh-mela.co.uk See p.179 for details.

September
Doors Open Day c/o Cockburn Association ☎0131/557 8686, ⓦwww.cockburnassociation.org.uk. Free. A great opportunity to visit a number of historically and architecturally interesting buildings, most of which are otherwise closed to the public. Venues change each year, but range from private houses to the Central Mosque. Normally takes place on the last Saturday in September.

November
St Andrew's Day Scotland's patron saint is commemorated on 30 November; controversially, it isn't a public holiday, although it is the one day of the year you can get free entrance to Edinburgh Castle.

December
Capital Christmas ⓦwww.edinburghschristmas.com. Of the various seasonal events lined up throughout December, most prominent is the huge ferris wheel beside the Scott Monument, with an outdoor skating rink installed nearby (see p.100).

December 31
Hogmanay ⓦwww.edinburghshogmanay.org. Hogmanay is the Scots' name for New Year's Eve, a unique mix of tradition, hedonism, sentimentality and enthusiasm. Its roots lie in ancient pagan festivities based around the winter solstice, which in most places gradually merged with Christmas; when hardline Scottish Protestant clerics abolished the Catholic mass of Christmas in the sixteenth century, the Scots, not wanting to miss out on a mid-winter knees-up, instead put their energy into greeting the New Year, a tradition which continues to this day. Edinburgh has established a reputation for hosting one of the liveliest parties, with (weather permitting) 100,000 people thronging the city centre to enjoy live bands, dancing, plenty of drinking and a massive fireworks display from the castle and other prominent landmarks at midnight. Passes to different parts of the event cost from £5, and are available on a first-come-first-served basis, from early October onwards, from the Hub on Castlehill (☎0131/473 2000) or via the website.

Directory

Airlines British Airways ☎0870/850 9850, ⓦwww.ba.com; British European ☎0871/522 6100, ⓦwww.flybe.com; British Midland ☎0870/607 0555, ⓦwww.flybmi.com; EasyJet ☎0870/600 0000, ⓦwww.easyjet.com; KLM ☎0870/507 4074, ⓦwww.klm.com.
Banks and exchange All the major UK banks have branches in central Edinburgh, with ATMs and currency exchange; the main concentrations are in the area between Hanover St and St Andrew Square in the east end of the central New Town. Post offices (see p.183) will exchange currency commission-free; you can also try Thomas Cook, 28 Frederick St (Mon–Sat 9am–5.30pm; ☎0845/308 9277); and currency exchange bureaus in the main tourist office (see p.172). To change money after hours, try one of the upmarket hotels – but expect a hefty commission charge.
Bike rental Although hilly, Edinburgh is a reasonably bike-friendly city with several cycle paths, all of which are detailed on the map published by local cycling action group Spokes (☎0131/313 2114, ⓦwww.spokes.org.uk). For rental, try Edinburgh

Fly Less – Stay Longer!

Rough Guides believes in the good that travel does, but we are deeply aware of the impact of fuel emissions on climate change. We recommend taking fewer trips and staying for longer. If you can avoid travelling by air, please use an alternative, especially for journeys of under 1000km/600miles. And always offset your travel at ⊛www.roughguides.com/climatechange.

Cycle Hire, just off the Royal Mile at 29 Blackfriars St (⊕0131/556 5560; ⊛www .cyclescotland.co.uk; £10–15 per day).

Car rental Arnold Clark, 38 Seafield Rd East⊕0844/844 3817, ⊛www .arnoldclarkrental.co.uk; Avis, 5 West Park Place ⊕0870/153 9103, ⊛www .avis.co.uk; Budget, Edinburgh Airport ⊕0131/333 1926, ⊛www.budget.co.uk; Europcar, 24 East London St ⊕0131/557 3456, ⊛www.europcar.co.uk; Hertz, 10 Picardy Place ⊕0131/556 8311, ⊛www .hertz.co.uk; Thrifty, 42 Haymarket Terrace ⊕0131/337 1319, ⊛www.thrifty.co.uk. Expect to pay around £20–25 per day for a basic car.

Car parking It is emphatically not a good idea to take a car into central Edinburgh: despite the presence of several expensive multistorey car parks, finding somewhere to park involves long and often fruitless searches. Street parking restrictions are draconian: residents' zone parking areas and double-yellow lines are no-go areas at all times, while cars parked for more than five minutes on single yellow lines or overdue parking-meter-controlled areas are likely to be fined £40 by one of the swarms of inspectors who patrol day and night. In severe cases cars can be towed away, with a retrieval fee of £120. Most ticket and parking-meter regulations cease at 6.30pm Monday to Friday, and at 1.30pm on Saturday.

Football Edinburgh's two Premier Division teams normally play at home to passion-ate crowds of around 10,000 on alternate weekends. Heart of Midlothian currently play at Tynecastle Stadium, Gorgie Rd (⊕0131/200 7201, ⊛www.heartsfc .co.uk), a couple of miles west of the centre. Hibernian play at Easter Rd Stadium (⊕0131/661 1875, ⊛www.hibs.co.uk), a mile northeast of the centre. Match tickets cost around £20.

Gay and lesbian contacts Gay and les-bian switchboard (Mon–Sun 7.30–10pm; ⊕0131/556 4049); Edinburgh LGBT Centre for Health and Wellbeing, 9 Howe St (⊕0131/523 1100; ⊛www.lgbthealth .org.uk).

Genealogical research General Register Office for Scotland ⊕0131/334 0380; ⊛www.scotlandspeople.gov.uk; Scottish Genealogy Society, 15 Victoria Terrace ⊕0131/220 3677, ⊛www .scotsgenealogy.com; Scottish Roots, 22 Forth St ⊕0131/477 8214, ⊛www .scottishroots.com.

Golf Edinburgh is awash with fine golf courses, but most are private. The best public 18-hole courses are the two on the Braid Hills (both on ⊕0131/447 6666).

Hospital Edinburgh's new Royal Infirmary at Little France, about four miles southeast of the city centre (⊕0131/536 1000), has a 24hr casualty department. There are also casualty departments at the Western General, two miles northwest of the centre on Crewe Road North ⊕0131/536 1000 (24hr); and for children at the Sick Kids' hospital, near the Meadows on Sciennes Rd ⊕0131/536 1000.

Internet There are plenty of places around Edinburgh where you can go online. Many hotels, guesthouses and hostels have facilities; in the centre of town try Electronic Corner, beside Platform 1 at Waverley Station (Mon–Fri 7.30am–9pm, Sat 8am–9pm, Sun 9am–9pm), or Internet Café, 98 West Bow (daily 10am–11pm) at the east end of the Grassmarket. The average cost for an hour's use is about £1.20–£2 per hour.

Left luggage Counter by platform 1 at Waverley Station (daily 7am–11pm; ⊕0131/558 3829).

Lost property Edinburgh Airport ⊕0870/040 0007; Edinburgh Police HQ ⊕0131/311 3141; Lothian Buses ⊕0131/558 8858; First Bus ⊕0870/872 7271; Scotrail ⊕0141/335 3276.

Money The basic unit of currency in Scot-land is the pound sterling (£), divided into 100 pence (p). Bank of England banknotes are legal tender in Scotland; in addition, the Bank of Scotland, the Royal Bank of Scotland and the Clydesdale Bank issue their own banknotes, including the now rare £1 notes. A number of shops and services (but by no means all) will accept payment in euros.

Opening hours Traditional shop hours are Monday to Saturday 9 or 10am to 5.30 or 6pm, but you'll find many of the city centre shops open on Sundays and later on Thursday and/or Friday evenings. The basic licensing hours for pubs are 11am–11pm daily, though most close later on Friday and Saturday nights and open later on Sundays. Restaurants are generally open at lunchtime from noon–2pm and in the evening from 7–10pm, though some are open longer hours or don't shut during the afternoon. The most common days for a restaurant to be closed are Sunday or Monday.

Pharmacy Boots, 48 Shandwick Place (☎0131/225 6757; Mon–Fri 8am–8pm, Sat 8am–6pm, Sun 10.30am–4.30pm).

Police In an emergency call 999. Otherwise contact the Force Communications Centre on ☎0131/311 3131.

Post office The largest post office in central Edinburgh is in the St James Centre at the east end of Princes St (Mon–Sat 9am–5.30pm, closed Sun; ☎0845/722 3344).

Swimming pools Edinburgh has one Olympic-standard modern pool, the Royal Commonwealth, at 21 Dalkeith Rd, Newington (☎0131/667 7211); and some considerably older pools, including Glenogle Rd in Stockbridge (☎0131/343 6376); and 6 Thirlestane Rd in Marchmont (☎0131/447 0052). For all opening hours and details of facilities follow the links to "Leisure" at ⊛www.edinburgh.gov.uk.

Tipping There are few fixed rules regarding tipping. Where you've received table service in a restaurant, 10 percent is typical for good service, though you should check that a service charge (10 to 12.5 percent) hasn't already been added to your bill. You are within your rights to delete this and pay a more appropriate sum.

ESSENTIALS Directory

Chronology

Edinburgh Chronology

c. 1000 BC ▸ First indications of inhabitation on Castle Rock.

80 AD ▸ Romans arrive in Scotland but bypass Edinburgh to establish a fort at Cramond.

6th Century ▸ Earliest documentary evidence of name Din Eidin ("fortress of the hill-slope"), capital of the Gododdin tribe of early Britons.

638 ▸ Northumbrians capture the city, renaming it Edinburgh.

1128 ▸ Holyrood Abbey founded by David I, who begins to regard Edinburgh rather than Dunfermline as the principal royal residence.

1513 ▸ Scots defeated by English at Flodden, prompting the building of a defensive wall around Edinburgh, completed in 1558.

1542 ▸ James V dies, leaving three-week-old daughter, Mary, as Queen of Scots.

1555 ▸ Protestant preacher John Knox returns from exile to become minister of St Giles.

1560 ▸ Reformation in Scotland replaces Catholicism with Calvinism.

1567 ▸ Mary deposed in favour of her son, James VI.

1582 ▸ University of Edinburgh founded.

1603 ▸ Union of Crowns; James VI departs Edinburgh for London to inherit crown of Elizabeth I and James become James I of England, Scotland and Ireland.

1638 ▸ National Covenant signed in Greyfriars' churchyard to defend church in Scotland against attempts by Charles I to impose Episcopalian system.

1681 ▸ Royal College of Physicians and Advocates' Library both established, marking Edinburgh as the centre of professional life in Scotland.

1695 ▸ William Paterson from Dumfries sets up Bank of Scotland, a year after founding the Bank of England.

1707 ▸ Union of Parliaments; Scottish Parliament dissolved in Edinburgh.

1745 ▸ Bonnie Prince Charlie occupies the Palace of Holyroodhouse during the Jacobite rebellion.

1766 ▸ Architect James Craig's plan for the New Town wins public competition.

1771 ▸ Tobias Smollet's description of Edinburgh as "a hot-bed of genius" summarizes the city's role in the Scottish Enlightenment, led by figures such as David Hume and Adam Smith.

1822 ▶ Visit of tartan-clad George IV to Edinburgh, stage-managed by Sir Walter Scott, is the first by a reigning monarch since Charles II.

1829 ▶ Execution of William Burke, partner of William Hare, the city's most famous bodysnatchers.

1836 ▶ Arrival of railway and canals in Edinburgh.

1850 ▶ Robert Louis Stevenson born in Howard Place, near Water of Leith.

1920 ▶ Leith incorporated into City of Edinburgh.

1947 ▶ Edinburgh hosts first International Festival.

1969 ▶ Maggie Smith wins Oscar for starring role in The Prime of Miss Jean Brodie.

1970 ▶ Commonwealth Games first held in Edinburgh.

1996 ▶ Stone of Destiny returned to Edinburgh Castle from Westminster Abbey.

1999 ▶ First Scottish general election since 1707. Scottish parliament re-established in Edinburgh.

2004 ▶ New Scottish Parliament building at Holyrood opens.

Travel store

Available from all good bookstores D: Rough Guide DIRECTIONS

For more information go to www.roughguides.com

- **Read** Rough Guides' trusted travel info

- **Access** exclusive articles from Rough Guides authors

- **Update** yourself on new books, maps, CDs and other products

- **Enter** our competitions and win travel prizes

- **Share** ideas, journals, photos & travel advice with other users

- **Earn** points every time you contribute to the Rough Guide community and get rewards

BROADEN YOUR HORIZONS

Listen Up!

"You may be used to the Rough Guide series being comprehensive, but nothing will prepare you for the exhaustive Rough Guide to World Music . . . one of our books of the year."

Sunday Times, London

Rough Guide Music Titles

The Beatles • Blues • Bob Dylan • Classical Music
Elvis • Frank Sinatra • Heavy Metal • Hip-Hop
iPods, iTunes & music online • Jazz • Book of Playlists
Led Zeppelin • Opera • Pink Floyd • Punk • Reggae
Rock • The Rolling Stones • Soul and R&B • World
Music Vol 1 & 2 • Velvet Underground

NOTES

small print & **Index**

SMALL PRINT

A Rough Guide to Rough Guides

In 1981, Mark Ellingham, a recent graduate in English from Bristol University, was travelling in Greece on a tiny budget and couldn't find the right guidebook. With a group of friends he wrote his own guide, combining a contemporary, journalistic style with a practical approach to travellers' needs. That first Rough Guide was a student scheme that became a publishing phenomenon. Today, Rough Guides include recommendations from shoestring to luxury and cover hundreds of destinations around the globe, including almost every country in the Americas and Europe, more than half of Africa and most of Asia and Australasia. Millions of readers relish Rough Guides' wit and inquisitiveness as much as their enthusiastic, critical approach and value-for-money ethos. The guides' ever-growing team of authors and photographers is spread all over the world.

In the early 1990s, Rough Guides branched out of travel, with the publication of Rough Guides to World Music, Classical Music and the Internet. All three have become benchmark titles in their fields, spearheading the publication of a range of more than 350 titles under the Rough Guide name, including phrasebooks, waterproof maps, music guides from Opera to Heavy Metal, reference works as diverse as Conspiracy Theories and Shakespeare, and popular culture books from iPods to Poker. Rough Guides also produce a series of more than 120 World Music CDs in partnership with World Music Network.

Visit www.roughguides.com to see our latest publications.

Rough Guide travel images are available for commercial licensing at www.roughguidespictures.com

Publishing information

This 2nd edition published March 2008 by
Rough Guides Ltd, 80 Strand, London WC2R 0RL.
345 Hudson St, 4th Floor, New York,
NY 10014, USA.

Distributed by the Penguin Group
Penguin Books Ltd, 80 Strand, London WC2R 0RL
Penguin Group (USA), 375 Hudson Street,
NY 10014, USA
14 Local Shopping Centre, Panchsheel Park, New
Delhi 110017, India
Penguin Group (Australia), 250 Camberwell Road,
Camberwell, Victoria 3124, Australia
Penguin Group (Canada), 10 Alcorn Avenue,
Toronto, ON M4V 1E4, Canada
Penguin Group (NZ), 67 Apollo Drive, Mairangi Bay,
Auckland 1310, New Zealand
Typeset in Bembo and Helvetica to an original
design by Henry Iles.
Cover concept by Peter Dyer.

Printed and bound in China
© Donald Reid 2008

No part of this book may be reproduced in any form
without permission from the publisher except for
the quotation of brief passages in reviews.
208pp includes index

A catalogue record for this book is available from
the British Library

ISBN 978-1-85828-373-9

The publishers and authors have done their best
to ensure the accuracy and currency of all the
information in Edinburgh DIRECTIONS, however,
they can accept no responsibility for any loss,
injury, or inconvenience sustained by any traveller
as a result of information or advice contained in
the guide.

1   3   5   7   9   8   6   4   2

Help us update

We've gone to a lot of effort to ensure that the 2nd edition of Edinburgh DIRECTIONS is accurate and up-to-date. However, things change – places get "discovered", opening hours are notoriously fickle, restaurants and rooms raise prices or lower standards. If you feel we've got it wrong or left something out, we'd like to know, and if you can remember the address, the price, the phone number, so much the better.

Please send your comments with the subject line "Edinburgh DIRECTIONS Update" to ✉mail@roughguides.com. We'll credit all contributions and send a copy of the next edition (or any other Rough Guide if you prefer) for the very best emails.
Have your questions answered and tell others about your trip at ⊕community.roughguides.com

Rough Guide credits

Text editor: Alison Murchie
Layout: Sachin Tanwar
Photography: Helena Smith
Cartography: Rajesh Mishra

Picture editor: Jj Luck
Proofreader: Anita Sach
Production: Rebecca Short
Cover design: Chloë Roberts

SMALL PRINT

The author

Donald Reid was brought up in Glasgow, studied in Edinburgh and left the country soon afterwards to avoid the threat of an office. He saw a bit of the world from the decks of yachts and fishing boats, jumped ship to hang out in Cape Town for a few years then returned to Scotland where he works as a freelance writer and editor specializing in food and drink.

Acknowledgements

The author would like to thank Claire Sawers and Duncan Forgan for their enthusiastic research and contributions, Helena for her pics and Alison for keeping us all roped up and bobbing on the surface. There are many around Edinburgh who have helped by opening doors, pointing the way, offering suggestions, providing information and serving coffee – your help and support are much appreciated. A dear Edinburgh friend, Penny Thomson, is sadly missed for she knew this city so well and offered much enthusiasm and insight. Most of all, thanks again to Mo, Riona and Fergus for showing me all that's best about being here.

The editor would like to thank Sachin for type setting, Anita for proofreading, Rajesh for the maps, Helena for lovely pics and Jj for choosing them, and Donald for being a pleasure to work with.

Readers' letters

Justyna Balowska, Andy Cox, Leslie Croce, Vicki Ong, Mrs J Scott.

Photo credits

All images © Rough Guides except the following:

Front cover image: Scottish Parliament Building © Mark Thomas
Back cover image: Calton Hill © Mark Thomas
p.4 Piper, Edinburgh © Jon Arnold Images/Alamy
p.5 National Monument on Calton Hill, Edinburgh © Brendan MacNeill/Alamy
p.5 Interior of National Portrait Gallery © Edinburgh/British Tourist Authority
p.6 View of Old Town © Scottish Viewpoint/Alamy
p.6 Café © Tips Images
p.7 Heriot Row in New Town © Iain Masterton/Alamy
p.8 View of Dean Village from Leith walk © Ingrid Rasmussen/British Tourist Authority
p.8 Holyrood Park © British Tourist Authority
p.11 Dugald Stewart Monument and cityscape © Michael McQueen
p.12 Doll's House, Edinburgh International Festival

© Richard Termine/Edinburgh International Festival 2007
p.12 Fireworks, Edinburgh International Festival © David Robertson/Alamy
p.13 Stand Up/Fringe Festival © Tom Stade/Fringe Festival
p.13 Book Festival, Edinburgh © europhotos/Alamy
p.15 Palace of Holyroodhouse © AA World Travel Library/Alamy
p.15 Mary, Queen of Scots, Clouet, François © The Royal Collection 2004, Her Majesty Queen Elizabeth II
p.18 Inchcolm Abbey, Inchcolm Island © Colin Woodbridge/Alamy
p.18 Abbey Ruins of Holyrood Palace © PBPA Paul Beard Photo Agency/Alamy
p.19 Gladstones Land © Worldwide Picture Library/Alamy

p.19 Canongate Kirk © Duncan Hale-Sutton

p.21 Calton Hill from the Calton Old Burial Ground © Duncan Hale-Sutton/Alamy

p.22 Scott Monument, Edinburgh © Mark Thomas/Alamy

p.24 The Fruitmarket Gallery © Alan Dimmick

p.25 Museum of Scotland © Natalie Pecht/British Tourist Authority

p.25 Interior of Royal Museum © Iain Masterton/Alamy

p.27 Golf © Getty Images

p.27 Loony Dook swim © Jeff J Mitchell/Getty Images

p.27 Murrayfield © Ian Stewart/AFP/Getty Images

p.30 Georgian dining room interior © National Trust For Scotland

p.35 Mary King's Close © Continuum Group

p.37 Falko Konditormeister – fruit petit fours © Robert Linton

p.41 Pride © Dave Patterson, Pride Scotia

p.44 Princes Street Gardens © doughoughton/Alamy

p.44 Taste of Edinburgh © Chris Watt

p.45 Beltane © Jim Richardson/Getty Images/National Geographic

p.45 Street party, Hogmanay © Alistair Linford/Alamy

p.45 Rugby fan, Murrayfield © Jonathan Littlejohn/Alamy

p.47 Royal Botanic Gardens © Scottish Viewpoint/Alamy

p.48 The outdoor terrace of Oloroso © Scottish Viewpoint/Alamy

p.49 Royal Botanic Gardens © mediacolor's/Alamy

p.52 Scottish Parliament © South West Images, Scotland/Alamy

p.110 Harvey Nichols, Edinburgh © Grant Smith 2005/Courtesy Harvey Nichols

p.145 Pentlands on a winter's day © Stock Images/Alamy

Index

Maps are marked in colour